WHAT PEOPLE ARE SAYING ABOUT

THE NATURALIST AND THE CHRIST

What does a suffering God have to do with Darwinian theory? In this five-session course, Tim Heaton brings the crisis of faith brought about by the death of Darwin's 10-year old daughter and the arguments subsequently developed in *The Origin of Species*, movingly captured in the film *Creation*, into dialogue with the traditional Lenten meditation on Jesus's temptation in the wilderness. The perspective is enriched by engaging with the writings of contemporary theologians and scientists.

This is a course for twenty-first century Christians and I commend it warmly.

The Rt Revd Stephen Conway, Bishop of Ely

An intriguing course for Lent which interweaves scripture and science, film and Christian thought, all in the context of discussion. It is carefully researched, elegantly written and well-presented.

The Rt Revd Dr Graham Kings, Bishop of Sherborne

I am very grateful to Tim for all the hard work and creativity he has put in to producing this course. Having read the course material myself I know that those groups who study it will be in for an exciting and challenging time. The issue of the environment and creation is clearly a very important one and I am sure that this course will open up many areas that will be fruitful and productive. I am convinced that we, as Christians, need to go back again to read our Bibles carefully and thoughtfully and I know that this course will encourage others to do this.

The Rt Revd Tim Thornton, Bishop o

I commend this Lent Course to parishes and groups who would like to deepen their understanding of one of those areas in Christian life where there remains sometimes irreconcilable differences in belief. It reminds us of the shock of Darwin's theory in his time, and gives us a feel for how Christians developed analytical tools to think afresh about what we believe. It is a thorough and thought-provoking course and a good addition to resources for a thoughtful Lent.

The Venerable Stephen Waine, Archdeacon of Dorset

I am struck by the substantial nature of this course. It is not light-weight – it tackles many profound issues and takes things seriously, using a lot of real theological material and references. No subject is glossed, no one is misrepresented, neither are important issues shirked. It's great to see a Lent study course which isn't patronizing or bland - this is genuinely an impressive piece of work. I am also struck throughout by the pleasantness of Heaton's style – he is entirely readable and never lets that slip.

The Revd Canon Edward Probert, Chancellor of Salisbury Cathedral

The Naturalist and the Christ

A Lent Course Based on the Film *Creation*

The Naturalist and the Christ

A Lent Course Based on the Film *Creation*

Tim Heaton

Winchester, UK
Washington, USA

First published by Circle Books, 2011
Circle Books is an imprint of John Hunt Publishing Ltd., Laurel House, Station Approach,
Alresford, Hants, SO24 9JH, UK
office1@o-books.net
www.o-books.com

For distributor details and how to order please visit the 'Ordering' section on our website.

Text copyright: Tim Heaton 2011

ISBN: 978 1 84694 762 9

A CIP catalogue record for this book is available from the British Library.

Design: Lee Nash

Printed in the UK by CPI Antony Rowe
Printed in the USA by Offset Paperback Mfrs, Inc

We operate a distinctive and ethical publishing philosophy in all
areas of our business, from our global network of authors to
production and worldwide distribution.

CONTENTS

In memory of my father
James Heaton
1930 – 2010

Just as we have borne the image of the man of dust,
we will also bear the image of the man of heaven
(1 Corinthians 15.49)

Acknowledgements

I owe my inspiration for writing this course to Hilary Brand. I have never met Hilary, but in 2009 my parish decided to do her Lent course *Christ and the Chocolaterie* (2002 Darton, Longman and Todd). It was a most refreshing course, unlike anything I had ever done before, and greatly enjoyed by all who participated in it. The secret of its appeal, I think, was that it was based on the film *Chocolat* and involved watching clips from the film which then became the focus of the group discussion. It was this visual dimension – 'the strength of an image' as Hilary called it – that made the course so much more interesting and accessible than all the purely written material that I had encountered previously. Fired up by this innovative approach, the parish decided the following year to do another of her Lent courses, *Not a Tame Lion* (2008 Darton, Longman and Todd), based on the films *The Lion, the Witch and the Wardrobe* and *Shadowlands*. If your church has not done these two Lent courses then I thoroughly recommend them to you.

Shortly afterwards my brother-in-law Anthony and his wife Antonia gave me the film *Creation* (2009 Ocean Pictures/HanWay Films/BBC Films). This absorbing and deeply moving British film raised many issues which I felt church groups, including my own, would benefit from exploring further, and this is the finished product.

Thanks are due to several people for helping me make it to the finishing line. My wife Arabella pored over the first draft of the manuscript, made many helpful suggestions, and gave me unstinting support and encouragement every step of the way. Thank you to David, Daphne, Eileen, Dave, Pam, Vera, Margaret and Arabella, who all did the course in Lent 2011, and whose useful comments and feedback on the experience helped to improve the text further.

Finally, thanks to all at John Hunt Publishing Ltd for producing, publishing and promoting this book.

Chapter One

Introduction

All Christians believe in a creator God. In the words of the Apostles' Creed we profess our faith in "God, the Father almighty, creator of heaven and earth". In the Nicene Creed – the one we usually say in church on Sundays – we are called to affirm this same belief in a few more words: "We believe in one God, the Father, the Almighty, maker of heaven and earth, of all that is, seen and unseen." This is not a belief that Christians can choose to discard or ignore. Like the incarnation and the resurrection it is a central tenet of the faith that we are called to uphold.

Where Christians disagree with each other, however, is over *how* God created heaven and earth and all that exists. The term 'creationist' is usually applied today to some Christians (as well as some Jews and Muslims) who believe that the universe and all living creatures were created by God in accordance with the accounts given in the Old Testament – a belief system referred to as 'creationism'. Some creationists believe that God made the universe and everything in it in six days, because this is what the Bible says in Genesis 1. Some also believe, citing Biblical evidence, that all of this happened less than 10,000 years ago. Some 'young-earth creationists' are even prepared to defend a calculation made by James Ussher in 1654 that Creation began at 9 a.m. on 26 October 4004 B.C.

Genesis 1 tells us that God created all the different fish and birds on the fifth day of Creation, and all the insects and animals on the sixth day – humankind being God's final endeavour on day six. (That Genesis 2 gives us a different order of events, placing the creation of Adam *before* all other living creatures, is something we can ignore for now). Both creation narratives suggest that God engaged in separate and innumerable acts of species creation. As the children's song goes:

> Who put the hump upon the camel?
> Who put the neck on the giraffe?
> Who put the tail upon the monkey?
> Who made hyenas laugh?
> Who made whales and snails and quails?
> Who made hogs and dogs and frogs?
> Who made bats and rats and cats?
> Who made everything?
> (Paul Booth, *Who Put the Colours in the Rainbow?*)

The answer is: 'God made all of these!' It is this Biblical notion that every living species was created by God separately and in its current form – 'special creation' as it is termed – that the scientific evidence for evolution rejects. Evolution is not a theory but scientific fact, because beyond any doubt the appearance of a new species can be linked directly to a similar but distinctly different species preceding it in time. Take, for example, the elephant. The three living species of elephants, Asian, African savanna, and African forest, have all arisen within the last two million years. The fossil record of their ancestors – more than twenty extinct species in all (the most recent being the mammoth which has also been found preserved in ice in Siberia) – goes back nearly 50 million years. Even a child who has watched *Jurassic Park* or seen the great dinosaur reconstructions in the Natural History Museum knows that life on earth was once very different from what it is today. Evolution really happened – and continues to happen – and we are the children of evolution too. The real question is: *how* has evolution occurred?

Evolutionary theories had been published before Darwin published his in 1859, notably by the French naturalist Jean-Baptiste Lamarck some 40 years earlier. Evolution (or 'descent with modification' as Darwin preferred to call it) was not a new idea, but Darwin's great contribution was to put forward an explanation for this modification, expounding the natural laws that drive the process of alteration and change. His theory of evolution 'by means of natural selection' – a plausible *mechanism* for evolution – was significantly different from anything seen before.

So species evolution is a fact not a theory, although how it occurs is less easy to prove. Let me make an analogy. We all know that our local High Street has 'evolved'. Where there used to be a butcher, a baker and a greengrocer there is now a computer shop, a charity shop and a vacant site. What was there before can be proven by photographic and other archive records, and what is there now can be observed. The High Street *has* changed. What is open to speculation, however, is how and why this change has occurred. It might be because no one wants to buy meat, bread, and vegetables anymore, and what the High Street really needs is a shop selling ready-meals. Alternatively, it might be because the butcher, the baker and the greengrocer were unable to sell or pass on their businesses when they retired because the younger generation simply doesn't want to be in retailing – we are no more 'a nation of shopkeepers'. The most common theory, however, is that it is all down to the dominance of the supermarket – the 'survival of the fittest'.

So it is with Darwin's theory of evolution by natural selection: it stands today as the most widely accepted and plausible mechanism for species evolution. Before going any further I think it would be helpful to say a bit more about 'natural selection' because it is the cornerstone of Darwin's species theory and the essential factor that differentiates it from other evolutionary theories. Natural selection, which arises from a struggle for existence combined with minute variation among the species, acts automatically to select out unsuccessful variations and reward successful ones. We will return to it in Chapter Two, but this is how Darwin summarized it in *The Origin of Species*:

It may be said that natural selection is daily and hourly scruti-
nising, throughout the world, every variation, even the
slightest; rejecting that which is bad, preserving, and adding
up all that is good; silently and insensibly working, whenever
and wherever opportunity offers, at the improvement of each
organic being in relation to its organic and inorganic conditions of life. We see nothing of these slow changes in progress,
until the hand of time has marked the long lapse of ages, and
then so imperfect is our view into long past geological ages,
that we only see that the forms of life are now different from
what they formerly were. (Darwin 1998:66)

The publication of *The Origin of Species* was "a public event
unprecedented in the history of science" (Miller 2002:12). To say
that it shook the foundations of the Church is not hyperbole. She
survived, of course, to proclaim the Holy Scriptures afresh to a
new generation, as is her calling. The effect that Darwin's speculation on species evolution (which he had begun some twenty
years earlier) had on his own faith – such as it was – was not
nearly so cataclysmic: he believed it was possible to be an ardent
believer in the Most High God who created and rules the
universe and, at the same time, an evolutionist. Evolution was
about improvement, progress, and ongoing changes for the good
leading towards perfection. What wounded his faith in the end,
as we shall see, was the death of his favourite daughter Annie in
Easter Week 1851, at the age of ten. But even that was not a fatal
blow, and Darwin died an agnostic not an atheist.

About the Course

This course, which is suitable for Christians of all denominations
and could easily be undertaken by an ecumenical group
comprising different traditions, is not an attack on Darwinism and
a defence of creationism. Neither is it the opposite of that, for I am

loath to think of it as an 'attack' on creationism either. Creationists have a viewpoint which I respect, though I do not share it.

What this course seeks to do is to find some common ground between God and evolution. Can evolution and God co-exist? If the answer is 'yes' then we are led into asking some further questions: why did the Victorian Church find it so hard to accept Darwin's theory? What implications does it have for the Church? Why do some Christians today still find it hard to accept that evolution is not a theory but scientific fact? If the answer, ultimately, comes down to their understanding of Scripture as being infallible or inerrant, this prompts us to ask some more questions: what is the authority or 'reliability' of Scripture? What do we mean when we say 'this is the word of the Lord'? Can we choose to believe some parts of the Bible and not others, either because we *can't* believe them (for example the creation narratives in Genesis 1 and 2) or because we simply don't *want* to believe them (for example that God slaughtered all the firstborn males in Egypt as recounted in Exodus 12)? These are all important questions, and by the end of the course I hope that you might have found some answers to them and be a more confident Christian as a result.

But that is by no means all that this course seeks to achieve. It also examines Darwin's own Christian beliefs – quite typical for a person of his time – and his religious struggles. Because of the kind of Christian he was, with limited faith and a particular understanding of God conditioned by the theology of his day, he could find no rhyme or reason for the existence of pain and suffering in the world, especially when it so decisively and convincingly entered his own world with Annie's painful and wretched death. He was not able to reconcile the reality of suffering with his particular understanding of God; the way in which he *knew* God gave him no resources for dealing with the tragic loss that came upon him that Easter in 1851. The Church of his day offered him little defence at all.

So how can it be any different for us? The answer is that we need to re-focus our attention on the crucified God, the God on the cross, the suffering God revealed in Jesus Christ. That is what we shall be doing as we journey together through Lent and Holy Week, a journey to the cross and the empty tomb beyond. From the Middle Ages, it became the custom for Christians to begin Lent by being marked in ash with the sign of the cross – the ashes traditionally being made from burnt palm crosses from the previous year's Palm Sunday. Many churches still do this on Ash Wednesday, the minister imposing the ashes with words such as these: "Remember that you are dust, and to dust you shall return. Turn away from sin and be faithful to Christ". I hope that you might have the opportunity to be 'ashed' in this way as you begin this season of Lent, to remind you of where the forty days are leading you.

The forty days of Lent, beginning on Ash Wednesday and ending on Easter Eve (not counting Sundays as every Sunday is a 'mini-Easter'), recall the forty days that Jesus spent in the wilderness being tempted by Satan. So it is that the characteristic notes of Lent are self-denial, self-examination, almsgiving, and penitence – as well as religious study as a way of preparing for Easter (baptism/renewal of baptismal vows or admission/re-admission to communion), which is maybe why you have under-taken to do this course. The story of the Temptation of Jesus is traditionally set as the gospel reading in churches on the First Sunday of Lent – the Sunday immediately following Ash Wednesday. For this reason I have taken Luke's narrative as a scriptural 'underpinning' for the course, grounding each weekly session in a segment of this story. This is how it goes (Luke 4.1-13):

Jesus, full of the Holy Spirit, returned from the Jordan and was led by the Spirit in the wilderness, where for forty days he was tempted by the devil. He ate nothing at all during those days, and when they were over, he was famished. The devil said to him, "If you are the Son of God, command this stone to become a loaf of bread." Jesus answered him, "It is written, 'One does not live by bread alone.' "

Then the devil led him up and showed him in an instant all the kingdoms of the world. And the devil said to him, "To you I will give their glory and all this authority; for it has been given over to me, and I give it to anyone I please. If you, then, will worship me, it will all be yours." Jesus answered him, "It is written, 'Worship the Lord your God, and serve only him.' "

Then the devil took him to Jerusalem, and placed him on the pinnacle of the temple, saying to him, "If you are the Son of God, throw yourself down from here, for it is written, 'He will command his angels concerning you, to protect you,' and 'On their hands they will bear you up, so that you will not dash your foot against a stone.' " Jesus answered him, "It is said, 'Do not put the Lord your God to the test.' " When the devil had finished every test, he departed from him until an opportune time.

The 'opportune time' of the devil's return comes later – in the plot to kill Jesus (Luke 22.3-6):

Then Satan entered into Judas called Iscariot, who was one of the twelve; he went away and conferred with the chief priests and officers of the temple police about how he might betray him to them. They were greatly pleased and agreed to give him money. So he consented and began to look for an opportunity to betray him to them when no crowd was present.

In this way Luke links the Temptation of Jesus with his Passion, binding the beginning of Lent to its ending (Holy Week). Holy Week is part of Lent, and so the theme of Christ's suffering – and ours – becomes a major theme in Weeks Four and Five of the course.

Darwin died in 1882 and was buried in Westminster Abbey. As a new century dawned, a new generation was born: a generation that was to witness two World Wars and the Holocaust in the passing of just thirty-one years. In no small part due to these events, the twentieth century also saw the development of a 'new orthodoxy' in Christian thought, as a new generation of theologians sought to address the involvement of God in the sufferings of humanity. The result is what we know today as a 'theology of the cross', an understanding of God not as powerful and almighty in heaven but weak and suffering in the world, a notion that would have seemed quite strange to Darwin (even though he had trained for ordination) and most other Christians of his time. Had Darwin himself been aware of such ideas on the nature of God, then Annie's death might not have had quite the same impact on his faith as it did.

So I end this book with a chapter entitled 'A Theology of a Suffering God', which I suggest you might like to read in Holy Week when you have finished doing the course, as a way of rounding things off and growing further in your relationship with God. It is worth keeping in mind, too, as we think during the course about Creation, that the events of Holy Week mark the occurrence of a *new* creation: on the sixth day (Good Friday) God's work in Christ was accomplished, and on the seventh day (the Sabbath/Easter Eve) God rested in the tomb.

How to Do the Course

The course comprises five group sessions of ninety minutes each. Each session involves watching two clips from the film *Creation*, which then become the focus for discussion. This absorbing and deeply moving British film, released in 2009 to mark the bicentenary of Darwin's birth and the 150th anniversary of the first publication of *The Origin of Species*, stars Paul Bettany as Darwin, Jennifer Connelly as his devoutly Christian wife Emma, and

Martha West as their beloved daughter Annie. The film is based on Randal Keynes' book, *Annie's Box*, about the life of his great-great-grandfather. For the avoidance of any confusion, where the film departs from the book or any other known facts about Darwin's life and work, we shall be adhering to the film.

Before each group session there is a small amount of reading for you to do (the 'Prelude'), which should help prepare you for some of the topics that come up for discussion in the group session. Here are a few ideas about how to do the course:

The first thing I want you to do is have some fun – don't confuse study with penance! Lent is about 'taking things on' (study and almsgiving) as well as 'giving things up' (austerity and self-denial). There's no reason at all why this course shouldn't be fun, an opportunity to spend some time in the company of others and in a relaxed and friendly environment. So try to enjoy the course, because then I think you will engage better with it and get more out of it in the end.

Try as best as you can to interact with the other people doing this course with you. More than anything else this means actively listening to what other people have to say, rather than always thinking about what you are going to say next. If you keep this in mind you will learn not only from what the course itself has to say but also from what your fellow participants have to say – and they will hopefully learn something from you. It goes without saying that this is the principal benefit of doing a Lent course as part of a church group, rather than simply reading a spiritual book as a purely private Lenten devotion.

Give everyone a chance to have their say. Some people need more time to think than others, or are naturally quieter and more reserved and need time to pluck up courage to say something in a group situation. Try to give them that time; don't feel that you have to blurt something out every time there is an awkward silence after a question has been asked, because you might be getting in just before them (again!) and denying them the opportunity to share with the group their views and experiences.

Treat everyone with consideration and interest. Respect other people's viewpoints even if you don't necessarily agree with them.

Remember that very often there is no right or wrong answer to the questions posed by this course – we are dealing here with great mysteries. Say what you want to say, and you might be uttering a most profound theological truth! And don't be scared by the word 'theology' – it simply means 'talk about God'. What we are doing on this course is talking about God – we are 'doing' theology.

Don't be afraid to ask questions, no matter how simple or difficult you think they are. There's a good chance that someone else wanted to ask the same question but was too afraid to ask, and they will thank you for asking it.

Read the 'Prelude' that begins each Week of the course before attending the group session: if you don't, you might find that you are a bit 'behind' the rest of the group and unable to participate fully in the discussion.

Having said that, don't read ahead. There are some questions I want you to try to find answers to before I attempt to answer them later in the course. Take each week as it comes and try not to read the whole course in Week One, however eager you are! If you do that, you might find yourself 'ahead' of the rest of the group and looking a bit smarter than everyone else.

Some of the things that are said in the group sessions will be best kept within the group; some painful, personal experiences are likely to be aired. Respect confidentiality, and remember that the things you hear are for your ears only: make the group sessions a safe place to be open and honest with each other. If you or someone close to you has lost a child, you will find Week Five of the course (when we watch Annie die) particularly difficult. If the loss has been recent and you feel unable to talk about it you might prefer to miss this session altogether. Otherwise, particpate as best as you can, and remember that your own experiences and emotions – should you choose to share them – will be greatly respected by the rest of the group. As throughout the whole course, speaking from experience will always be more valuable to the group than speaking in a purely theoretical way.

Finally, try to 'frame' the course within the worship offered by your church during Lent. I have already mentioned Ash Wednesday as a way of marking the start of the course, but do try also to get to church on Maundy Thursday and Good Friday after the course has ended. I've always found it rather strange that many people in my church – who show up every Sunday without fail – don't attend on these most holy of Holy Days. Easter Day, when it arrives in all its glory, will be even more special if you do.

So perhaps, before we begin, we can draw up 10 'Rules of Engagement'. At the start of the first group session you will be asked to confirm that you have read them and that you agree to them:

Rules of Engagement

1. I will have some fun!
2. I will try to learn something from everyone in the group.
3. I will give everyone else a chance to have their say.
4. I will respect other people's viewpoints even if I disagree.
5. I will try to 'do' some theology.
6. I won't be afraid to ask questions.
7. I will read the 'Prelude' before each group session.
8. I won't read too far ahead.
9. I will keep confidential the things that I hear in the group.
10. I will try to get to church as often as I can in Lent and Holy Week.

If you are going to be a group leader please read on. If not, skip to the next chapter, 'A Brief Biography of Charles Darwin'. Read this, then the 'Prelude' to Week One, before the first group session. Bring a Bible with you to the group sessions, and remember – enjoy it!

A Guide for Leaders

The course comprises five group sessions of ninety minutes each, which ideally should be held at the same time each week for five weeks. It is advisable to run each session more than once, e.g. morning, afternoon, and evening, to give people the chance of attending when it suits them best. If you expect that large numbers will want to do the course, you will need to lay on multiple sessions to keep each group to a manageable size. A good group size, in my experience, is 10-20 people; anything less than this can be off-putting for those who want to 'keep a low profile', and with more than this it is hard for everyone to have the chance to participate fully.

Before the Course

Well in advance, and together with others who are going to be group leaders, decide on the dates and times for the course. Ideally, start the course in the week immediately following Ash Wednesday, and get a session in each week (Lent 1 – Lent 5) so as to finish before the start of Holy Week. Check for any clashes with other important local events: if the village pantomime is coming up and everyone in the community is either going to be in it or watching it, avoid clashing with rehearsal and perfor-mance times – you are likely to be the loser!

Choose the venue(s), check availability, and book them. The church hall is fine, so long as it is warm (heating *will* be required!), but if someone is willing to offer their home then I think this provides an altogether more friendly and comfortable setting. The room needs to be large enough to accommodate the group around a large TV set (or a screen if you are using a video projector).

Advertise the course as widely as you can – on posters, in your church and community magazines, pew sheets, and from the pulpit. Try to whip up some excitement and enthusiasm about the course, and make a point of inviting people who have not done a Lent course before: many church members think 'that's not something I do', and it's necessary to try to break that mindset.

Ask people to 'sign up' to the course – and which particular day/time in the week they want to come – rather than have them simply turn up on the day. You will need to know *in advance* the numbers attending so that you can buy and distribute sufficient copies of this book before the course begins (there is important reading to do before the first group session). Also, if the evening session is getting very full, then you will be able to lay on an additional evening session to keep the groups to a manageable size.

Buy the right number of copies of this book from your usual bookshop or from <www.circle-books.net>. Couples doing the course will probably want to share a copy rather than have one each – especially if you are asking them to pay for it! Decide whether you are going to ask participants to pay, or whether the church will either pay completely or subsidize the cost. Distribute the books *before* the start of the course so that participants have a chance to read what they have to read before the first group session, but bring some spare books along to the first session just in case.

Buy a copy of the DVD *Creation* from your usual DVD store. It may be useful to have more than one copy if you are holding several sessions each week with different leaders and in multiple locations.

Source the equipment you need. The TV set obviously needs

to be the largest you can lay your hands on – probably not less than 32" even for a small group, but the bigger the better. The DVD player should, if possible, have a time counter display (which some smaller machines do not) so that you can find more easily the start and end points of each film clip. These are given in the table 'Film Clip Start and End Points'. You will also need a flipchart (or whiteboard) and pens.

It is not essential that participants watch the whole film before starting the course, but they might find it helpful to do so: consider arranging a viewing of the film before the course begins – with popcorn and drinks of course!

Encourage participants to go to church on Ash Wednesday as a way of marking the start of the course – with or without the imposition of ashes – and perhaps distribute the books to them as they leave. Those who have not signed up to do the course may feel they are missing out on something and decide to join a group after all.

During the Course

Don't worry if you have never led a group before. You are not expected to know all the answers, and often there is no right or wrong answer. Your role is simply to 'facilitate' the group – to get discussion going and to keep the session moving along. Let others do the talking, and only chip in yourself if the discussion stalls or if you need to bring the conversation back on the right track. Give everyone the chance to respond to what they have seen and heard, and the opportunity to ask questions. If you cannot answer a question thrown your way don't try to 'bluff it': admit ignorance or, better still, get someone else to answer it! Try not to impose your own ideas too often, or answer your own questions. Remember that you are the host, so try to make everyone feel welcome, comfortable, and relaxed.

Above all, keep an eye on the clock. The best way to ensure that no one comes back for the second session is to run overtime or finish the ninety minutes having only tackled the first question! The timings suggested for each part of the session – and the clock in the left margin – should help you keep things on track. You must, of course, allow some flexibility, but be firm when necessary in moving on to the next item. It may mean bringing to an end a vibrant conversation when it is clear that people still have things they are bursting to say, but this is an important part of your role as leader.

You may wish to start each group session with a prayer. Each session then follows the same symmetrical pattern, which looks like this:

Group Session

0.00	Bible Study	10 minutes
0.10	Film Clip 1	5 minutes
0.15	Brainstorm	5 minutes
0.20	Group Discussion	10 minutes
0.30	In Small Groups	10 minutes
0.40	Feedback and Share	5 minutes

HALF TIME

0.45	Film Clip 2	5 minutes
0.50	Brainstorm	5 minutes
0.55	Group Discussion	10 minutes
1.05	In Small Groups	10 minutes
1.15	Feedback and Share	5 minutes
1.20	Meditation and Prayer	10 minutes

Bible Study
This is time for the group to think and talk about the Bible passage that begins the Prelude to each weekly session. Aim to make some connections between the 'word' and the 'world',

understanding not only the passage and its context but also how it applies to our present situation and experience. (In Week One this time is used instead as a period of welcome and introduction).

Film Clip
Show the film clip, using the guide below to find the right start and end points:

Film Clip Start and End Points

WEEK 1   **Film Clip 1**
Start Scene 5. FF to 0.28. Start at scene of hunters approaching through the grass.
End After Annie says, "I like it, it makes me cry" (0.33).
Film Clip 2
Start Scene 2. FF to 0.10. Start at "October 17th 1858."
End After Huxley says, "Come on, Hooker, it'll be dark soon" (0.15).

WEEK 2   **Film Clip 1**
Start At the beginning of Scene 6 (0.33, Darwin in bed).
End After Annie's second cartwheel on the beach (0.37).
Film Clip 2
Start At the beginning of Scene 7 (0.39, church service).
End After Annie says, "The fox has to eat the rabbit otherwise the fox's babies will die" (0.44).

WEEK 3   **Film Clip 1**
Start Scene 1. FF to 0.02. Start at "In Tierra Del Fuego, a land of fire..."
End After the upside-down image of Annie with the clock striking in the background (0.07).

Film Clip 2
Start Scene 9. FF to 0.55. Start at "Post for you, Sir – this one's from the Spice Islands."
End After Darwin collapses on the ground and his butler says, "Help me here, help me here!" (1.01).

WEEK 4   **Film Clip 1**
Start At the beginning of Scene 4 (0.20, children running through the field).
End After Darwin wakes from his dream with a start and pulls the blanket up around him (0.24).
Film Clip 2
Start Scene 11. FF to 1.06. Start at scene of Darwin being scrubbed in the bath.
End After Darwin finishes his prayer, "Thank you – Amen" (1.10).

WEEK 5   **Film Clip 1**
Start At the beginning of Scene 13 (1.17, Darwin entering Annie's room).
End After the scene changes to autumn colours (1.22).
Film Clip 2
Start At the beginning of Scene 12 (1.10, Darwin in Gully's office).
End After Darwin walks out of Gully's office (1.14).
N.B. Not when you see the horse and trap – the scene returns later to Gully's office.

Brainstorm
Having watched the film clip, have the group say whatever is on their minds and write some of these things up on a flipchart or whiteboard. If the subsequent discussions stall and people run out of things to say, you can always come back to these points later to help things along.

Group Discussion
This is for the whole group to discuss as one. Give everyone the freedom to speak; be aware of a few people dominating the conversation and try to give as many people as possible the chance to be heard. Aim to encourage and affirm every participant and bring everyone into the discussion, but don't put undue pressure on those who would rather remain silent. Welcome any contribution from a quieter member. If the discussion stalls, go back to something that came up in the brainstorming.

In Small Groups
Divide the group into small groups of 3 or 4: this is preferable to pairs because some people find it quite awkward being one-to-one. People who were a little reticent about speaking up in the group discussion (or who didn't get a chance!) will now have the opportunity to contribute something. Keep the small groups the same in subsequent sessions as they will get to bond with each other and feel that they are in 'a safe place'. When people break into small groups for the first time in each session, this is your chance to set the DVD to the right place for film clip 2.

Feedback and Share
Call the group back together and invite each small group to feedback and share what they have been discussing. Let them know that they don't have to feedback everything, as they may prefer to keep some of the things they have talked about to themselves rather than share them with others.

Meditation and Prayer
Each session ends with ten minutes of readings, meditation and prayer. Ask for four volunteers to read the readings and the closing prayer. Never impose a reading on somebody, and only read yourself if there are no volunteers.

After the Course

Encourage participants to go to church as often as they can in Holy Week – especially on Palm Sunday, Maundy Thursday, and Good Friday. It may be possible to link some of the course material/themes to these services.

Consider keeping the group going when the course has ended, after a suitable break, to continue meeting regularly for Bible study, prayer, and fellowship. It may be a good idea to sound people out about this in the final group session. If participants have enjoyed the course and bonded well together, you may be surprised at how many will want to go on meeting together in this way in the future.

Chapter Two

A Brief Biography of Charles Darwin

This is the story of one man's journey with God from the cradle to the grave. It started well enough: a solid Christian upbringing, training for ordination in the Church of England, and a place on a hydrographical and missionary voyage to South America. But in the fifteen years between his return from the *Beagle* voyage and the death of his daughter Annie, Darwin came to distrust the faith he had previously held. A number of intellectual doubts came to impinge on his beliefs but, above all, it was 'the problem of pain' (to borrow the title of C. S. Lewis' famous work of 1940) that left the deepest mark. Nevertheless, in the next thirty years until his death, during which he wrote a number of books as well as an autobiographical memoir, he never became an atheist. Whilst writing *The Origin of Species*, "possibly the most revolutionary work of the modern scientific imagination" (Wallace in Darwin 1998:viii), he still described himself as a 'theist' and towards the end of his life, when he did start to doubt the grounds for his belief in a creator God, he became an agnostic – someone who thinks that nothing can be known about the existence or nature of God. He believed the whole subject to be beyond the scope of human intellect. He stood in awe before the mystery of life, and the solution of the riddle lay beyond his mental reach. In a letter to John Fordyce in 1879 he wrote:

In my most extreme fluctuations I have never been an atheist in the sense of denying the existence of a God. – I think that generally (& more and more so as I grow older) but not always, that an agnostic would be the most correct description of my state of mind. (Darwin Correspondence Project. www.darwinproject.ac.uk/entry-12041)

And in his *Autobiography*, musing on the source of life:

I cannot pretend to throw the least light on such abstruse problems. The mystery of the beginning of all things is insoluble by us; and I for one must be content to remain an Agnostic. (The Complete Works of Charles Darwin Online. www.darwin-online.org.uk)

From Birth to the *Beagle*

Charles Robert Darwin was born in Shrewsbury on 12 February 1809, the fourth of five children born to Robert and Susannah Darwin. Susannah's father was Josiah Wedgwood, the illustrious Potteries magnate. He was a Unitarian Christian, a denomination established in central and eastern Europe in the post-Reformation years which developed in England in the seventeenth and eighteenth centuries. (Unitarianism holds to a belief in the unity of God and rejects the doctrine of the Trinity).

Robert was a wealthy country doctor and a man of little religious faith – a 'nominal' member of the Church of England. Susannah attended Unitarian chapel meetings, and Darwin himself began being tutored by a Unitarian minister when he was eight years old. But that same year his mother died, and his eldest sister Caroline took charge of his education, taking him from the Unitarian chapel back to the parish church at which he had been baptized.

The following year Darwin joined his older brother Erasmus (who had been named after their paternal grandfather, an early evolutionist) at Shrewsbury School, attending as a boarder despite the school being less than a mile from home, during which time he developed a keen interest in nature and collecting specimens. He remained there until he was sixteen, at which time his father sent him to study medicine at Edinburgh University – again in the footsteps of his brother Erasmus. Darwin never took to medicine. He gave up his medical studies partly because he was so distressed by the suffering of patients undergoing operations without anaesthetic, but two years at Edinburgh brought him into the world of science and a culture in which religious scepticism was intellectually possible. There he met a Scottish physician and evolutionist, Robert Grant, an expert on marine invertebrates, who believed that all life had evolved from the simplest algae; they became friends and often walked together the coastline around Edinburgh, observing the fauna of the seashore and discussing evolution. Talk of evolution – or 'transmutation' as it was then more commonly known – was considered scandalous by the religious establishment; it was even condemned by the scientific authorities of the day, the world of science being largely populated by the wealthy and educated clergy. Nevertheless, some freethinking radicals, such as the botanist and clergyman the Reverend William Herbert, were early evolutionary theorists.

For Darwin himself, however, such thoughts were to be put on hold. Because he wasn't getting on with medicine and seemed unlikely to follow his father into the profession, his father suggested ordination. The fact that Darwin had no clear or genuine calling to the priesthood was not a problem! It would be today, of course, but in the nineteenth century it was not. The life of an Anglican clergyman in those days offered eminent social status, comfort, and leisure, and many found the time to combine scientific study with their clerical duties. So in 1828, shortly before his nineteenth birthday, Darwin went up to Christ's College, Cambridge, to read Divinity and prepare for Holy Orders.

Like much of the English educational system at the time, Cambridge University was grounded in and governed by

Anglicanism. All students were required to declare their belief in the thirty-nine Articles of Religion and all Fellows were in Holy Orders. The theology Darwin actually read there is something we shall return to in Week Three of the course, for it is what formed him into the kind of Christian he was – one whose faith was vulnerable when tragedy struck. It was in many respects deficient, already somewhat outdated and, above all, had little to do with Jesus Christ and even less with the activity of the Holy Spirit. It centered on 'natural theology', the search for knowledge of God through the exercise of reason and the inspection of the world.

Natural theology holds to the idea that the natural world acts as a window into the character and purposes of God, that the God who made the world can be known through the world that he created. Importantly, it predicated itself upon the assumption that the world is a benign and well-ordered world, the work of a beneficent Creator, 'a happy world of delighted existence' to paraphrase the Reverend William Paley, whose *Natural Theology* (1802) particularly impressed Darwin at the time. The hymn *All things bright and beautiful*, written in 1848 and possibly inspired by Paley, expresses the same sentiment: 'how great is God Almighty, who has made all things well.' That nature was at heart benign had become one of the presumptions of the age.

Alongside his theological studies Darwin found ample time to indulge his passion for researching plant and insect life. He became a lifelong friend of the Reverend John Henslow, professor of botany and a model of the Victorian clergyman-naturalist that Darwin might one day emulate, and by the time he received his BA in Divinity in 1831 he was already planning an expedition to the Canary Islands to study its natural history.

This expedition never got underway, for an even more attractive adventure soon presented itself to Darwin: a certain Captain Robert Fitzroy was about to take a ship, *HMS Beagle*, around South America. He was aiming to complete a task started

23

some years earlier by Captain Pringle Stokes who had begun charting the coastal waters around the continent in order to improve Britain's trade and commerce with the region. It proved to be a terrible undertaking: appalling weather, unreliable maps, and an outbreak of scurvy amongst the crew. It all became too much for him and Stokes shot himself. Fitzroy, who was on the voyage with Stokes, took command of the vessel and steered the *Beagle* home.

Fitzroy was asked by the Admiralty to return and continue the work. Naturally he was wary, but he decided the voyage would be bearable if he could take with him a naturalist and companion with whom he could dine, converse, and share quarters. Darwin was approached (on Henslow's recommendation) and agreed to go. Not only did it excite his interest in natural history but, with ordination still a prospect, he believed the voyage would be of positive benefit to his clerical future: part of its purpose was to take the Reverend Richard Matthews to set up a Christian mission on the Tierra del Fuego archipelago.

The *Beagle* sailed from Plymouth on 27 December 1831 on a voyage around the world that would last for nearly five years. It did little to alter his Christian faith – such as it was – for better or for worse. Although the mission to the Fuegians was a disaster (we will see this in Week Three of the course), his several encounters with missionaries in the South Pacific greatly impressed him. He recognized that their work had a beneficial moral impact on society, and he came to view Christianity as a thoroughly decent, civilizing force and a fine British export! But other experiences on the voyage also raised some questions in his mind about some of things he had learned at Cambridge. In particular, whilst the *Beagle* was surveying the Chilean coast, Darwin witnessed both a volcanic eruption and a violent earthquake. The destruction and devastation he saw suggested to Darwin that nature had another side to it – one not at all benign and seemingly indifferent to human life – and it cast some considerable doubt on the 'happy world of delighted existence' he had read about in the comfort and security of his Cambridge rooms. Perhaps God Almighty had not 'made all things well.'

The Problem of Pain

When the *Beagle* returned on 2 October 1836, Darwin set about writing an account of the voyage and analyzing the many specimens he had brought back with him. All plans for ordination were cancelled. Motivated particularly by his observations of the marked differences of appearance and behaviour between the different types of finch found on the separate islands of the Galapagos archipelago (he doubted that the finches were all special creations of God), he also began to speculate on the origin of species, 'that mystery of mysteries' as he came to refer to it, writing down his thoughts and ideas in a series of notebooks that would later form the basis of his theory. He believed that the variations between the different finches were the raw material for natural selection. Such speculation did not destroy his belief in God: whilst he could no longer believe in special creation he saw the alternative of evolution as a grander and more dignified vision of God. A view of God capable of causing improvement of form in the organic world so that creatures could adapt and survive was an altogether more noble and glorious conception of God. Darwin's God was not in any way diminished by natural laws acting on creation to produce changes for the good of the species.

A visit to the Zoological Society in London in 1838 and an encounter with an orangutan named 'Jenny' (we will see this in Week One of the course) reinforced his belief that human beings were closely related to other primates. In short, all life was interrelated, humans were also creatures, and this is why talk of evolution had such serious implications for the Church. It wasn't simply the matter of saying that scripture was wrong. The real problem stemmed from the fact that the course of evolution is inherently unpredictable – it works in unforeseeable ways because the mutations and genetic interactions that drive evolution by producing variation are themselves unpredictable. Biological history turns on these tiny uncertainties. If we wound back the clock and started the evolutionary history of the world all over again, it would turn out differently from how it has this time. Humans would not be where and how we are now because we are simply the product of indeterminate chance. How, then, can it be said that we are the *intentional* creations of a loving God who meant us to be here – as we are now – created in his image? Doesn't evolution rule out any notion of divine purpose behind human life? Evolution struck at the dignity of humankind and called into question its conscious feeling of superiority.

Evolution also seemed to strike directly at the fundamental assumptions of a Church built on the moral absolutes of good and evil. The Church was in the business of saving souls – saving human beings who had all (each and every one of us according to St Augustine) been *born* sinners, having inherited the guilt of 'original sin' when Adam and Eve fell from grace. But if humanity never did actually hold a position of primal innocence in the first place – having evolved from anthropoid apes only in the very recent history of the world – then there can have been no 'Fall'. And if there was no Fall, how can it be said that Christ came to 'undo' the effects of original sin? Why then *did* God become man and die upon a cross if it was not to effect a reversal of the Fall?

Another argument might go like this: if the knowledge of good and evil cannot be located in the Fall, it must have developed as a natural instinct in human beings. If human beings are simply animals among other animals, sharing a common nature and mental qualities and having a mind that has developed from the mind of the lower animals, is it not possible that other sentient beings could have developed the same instinct and also be capable of choosing evil over good? If 'the wages of sin is death' (Romans 6.23), are not animals also in need of being saved from death? Why should the human race hold such a unique place in God's plan for salvation? We will return to these questions in Weeks Four and Five of the course, but let it be said for now that these and other questions are ones to which the Victorian Church struggled to find answers. Although some prominent Christian thinkers such as the Reverend Charles Kingsley and the Reverend Frederick Temple (later to become Archbishop of Canterbury 1896-1902) were able to accommodate the implications of evolution with Christianity, it wasn't really until the twentieth century that evolutionary theory became properly accepted – in most circles at least – in religious thought.

Now in his late twenties, Darwin began thinking about marriage, and on 29 January 1839 he married Emma Wedgwood, his first cousin on his mother's side and a devout Christian. The same year he published *Voyage of the Beagle* and their first child, William, was born. Anne ('Annie') followed in 1841, and in 1842 Darwin completed the first preliminary sketch of his theory. This 1842 sketch was followed by a second, longer one in 1844, which Darwin asked Emma to have published in the event of his sudden death.

Their London terrace home was now becoming unsuitable for the growing family, and so the Darwins moved to Down House, a former parsonage in the village of Downe near Bromley in Kent. In 1843, soon after the family arrived in their new home, their third child, Mary, was born, but she survived for only three weeks. Beyond the expected agony of grief, Mary's death appeared not to affect Darwin unduly – as Annie's death would certainly do. (Charles and Emma went on to have a further seven children, the last of whom, Charles, would also die in infancy).

In the 1840s Darwin's own health began to deteriorate. Having first fallen ill whilst on the *Beagle*, he suffered from a debilitating sickness that caused migraine, nausea, and acute vomiting, periodic in nature but sometimes lasting for months at a time. His health was often directly affected by his state of mind, and his nervous system began to be affected so that his hands trembled. This mysterious illness significantly worsened after his father's death in 1848 and he began to seek medical advice. Conventional methods had no effect on his symptoms so Darwin turned to hydrotherapy, a fashionable treatment of disease at the time in which water is used externally. In March 1849 Darwin moved his entire household – Emma, butler, maids, six children and their governess – to Malvern, where for three months he underwent water treatment at the hands of a renowned hydrotherapist, Dr. James Gully. It appeared to have some beneficial effect.

The same year, Darwin's three daughters, Annie, Henrietta, and Elizabeth, all contracted scarlet fever, an acute contagious disease characterized by fever, inflammation of the nose and throat, and a reddish skin rash. Henrietta and Elizabeth recovered well, but Annie seemed never to recover fully, resulting in long-term effects on her health. Through 1850, her condition deteriorated, and in March 1851, fearing that she might have inherited his stomach problems and convinced of the benefits hydrotherapy had had on his own illness, Darwin took her to Malvern for water treatment by Dr. Gully (we will see this in Week Four of the course).

He stayed until the end of March before returning to Downe, leaving Annie with her nurse, her governess, and her sister Henrietta. But two weeks later he received an urgent message from Malvern that Annie's condition had worsened: she was weak, exhausted, and vomiting badly. Darwin raced back and arrived on Maundy Thursday. In the night she deteriorated further; she was only semi-conscious, her pulse became weak and irregular, and Gully feared that she was dying. But she survived the night, and Good Friday, and by Easter Eve it looked as though she had turned the corner. Gully believed she would recover, but on Easter Day she took another turn for the worse. By Tuesday diarrhoea had set in, her breathing was shallow, and she slipped into unconsciousness. She died on Wednesday, 23 April 1851, at the age of ten. The death certificate recorded 'bilious fever with typhoid character', probably tuberculosis (known then as consumption), which accounted for between a quarter and a third of all deaths in England at the time and for which there was no known cure. Twenty years later in *The Descent of Man* (1871) Darwin noted that humans shared consumption with monkeys, and saw the point as proof of a common origin.

Darwin was devastated by Annie's death. 'She was my favourite child', he wrote a week later in a letter to William Fox, his second cousin and lifelong friend. She was not the first child he had lost, nor would she be the last, but her passing was unbearable and nothing would ever be the same again. He had watched her short and innocent life ebb away, and he had witnessed every moment of her wretched and undignified death. It did not make him deny the existence of God, and he had no belief that there was any Divine purpose behind it (as Emma did), but it did make him question whether a world of such endless suffering could possibly be grounded in, and guided by, a good and righteous God. He still firmly believed in a Divine Creator but had no faith in his infinite goodness.

Pen to Paper

Darwin's species sketches of 1842 and 1844, when he wrote them, were never intended for publication. These manuscripts would have been considered scandalous, the Devil's work, hugely controversial for their time, and Darwin never felt much at home as a revolutionary scientist. He wished to cause no offence to the religiously-minded (least of all his wife Emma whose Christian convictions were as strong as ever) or public outcry. He was also reluctant to publish until he felt confident in his ability to cope with the close scrutiny to which his argument was certain to be subjected and so they were put away while he carried on with other work. In 1846 he returned to his passion for nature and collecting specimens, and embarked upon a long and detailed study of barnacles, living and fossilized, that would last for the next eight years. His findings from this meticulous examination of one sea creature, that all had evolved by variation from a common ancestral form, did much to boost his confidence that his theory was sound. The Royal Society recognized the importance of this work by awarding him the Royal Medal in 1853.

By 1854, when his barnacles work was completed, public attitudes were beginning to change. Other evolutionary theories had been published, such as Robert Chambers' *Vestiges of the Natural History of Creation* (1844), and much of the public anger had already been vented. Evolutionary ideas were now securely in the public domain and, though still controversial, could be discussed openly and without the fear of outrage in a way that would have been impossible a decade earlier.

In 1856, encouraged by his friend the influential Scottish geologist Sir Charles Lyell (whose own three-volume magnum opus *Principles of Geology* (1830-33) had rejected the Biblical earth-span of 6,000 years), Darwin began to perfect his species theory and started writing it up in minute detail in a massive book to be called 'Natural Selection'. In 1858, however, when it was only half completed, he received a twenty-page letter from Alfred Russel Wallace, a naturalist and collector, outlining an evolutionary theory entitled 'On the tendency of varieties to depart indefinitely from the original type'. It was an identical theory of evolution! Darwin was shocked, fearing that the originality of his life's work would be lost, but he nevertheless forwarded it to Lyell as Wallace had requested. Lyell and another friend, Joseph Hooker, a botanist and director of the Royal Botanic Gardens in Kew, advised Darwin that he had a moral duty to send Wallace's manuscript for publication.

The solution, they suggested, would be for Darwin to produce a summary of his theory and for both papers to be published simultaneously. With some reservation Darwin agreed. Fortuitously, he had already written a short version of his species theory, which he had previously sent to his friend Asa Gray, Professor of Natural History at Harvard University. He named this paper 'On the Tendency of Species to form Varieties; and on the Perpetuation of Varieties and Species by Natural Means of Selection'. On 1 July 1858 the two papers, Darwin's and Wallace's, were presented together by Lyell and Hooker at a meeting of the Linnean Society in London, a publisher of natural history journals named after the eighteenth-century Swedish naturalist Carolus Linnaeus. Darwin himself did not attend the meeting (two days earlier his tenth child Charles had died from scarlet fever at the age of two years), and both papers were received without fanfare or public attention. (The Linnean Society continues today to award the Darwin-Wallace Medal for major advances in evolutionary biology).

It was in this surprisingly modest and unexciting way that Darwin's theory of evolution by natural selection – 'the single best idea anyone has ever had' (Dennett 1995:21) – came to see the light of day. Lest he be upstaged once more as a result of his slow and meticulous professionalism, it was clear that Darwin needed to publish his work without further delay, and he immediately set about producing a hastily-written abstract of his lengthy ongoing work 'Natural Selection'. This became *The Origin of Species* and was published on 24 November 1859. (A word of explanation here: *The Origin of Species* has become the commonly-used abbreviated title of this work, although it was originally published as *On the Origin of Species by Means of Natural Selection or, The Preservation of Favoured Races in the Struggle for Life*. Modern reprints of the book will be found under both titles – it is the same book).

The Origin of Species immediately became a widely talked about best-seller. Darwin had set out his theory in the first four chapters, four building blocks of what he called 'one long argument', which went something like this:

The Theory Outlined

Chapter 1: Variation under Domestication

Domesticated plants and animals show an enormous range of variation. Darwin kept and studied domestic pigeons, and found the diversity of the many breeds (their beaks, wings, tails, feet etc.) to be 'something astonishing'. Great as the differences are, all these varieties are descended from one species, the rock pigeon (*Columba livia*). Plant and animal breeders deliberately select variation, which Darwin called 'artificial selection'.

Chapter 2: Variation under Nature

A similar variation exists in nature among wild species. This variation is so great that naturalists are often unsure whether two types of a particular plant or animal are two different species or merely varieties of one; arguments over exactly how different they have to be to constitute separate species are common, and the difference between species and varieties is only a matter of degree. (How this individual variation/heredity occurs is not something Darwin could precisely account for; today we would call this mechanism 'genetics', but this science was not available to Darwin at the time).

Chapter 3: Struggle for Existence

All living things are engaged in a struggle for existence. The natural rate of increase of all living things is so great that (if unchecked) they would overwhelm the earth. Many more are propagated than can possibly survive, and so there is a struggle for existence among them and only a few progeny survive. This struggle is greatest among individuals of the same species, because each one needs exactly the same resources as the next in order to survive.

Chapter 4: Natural Selection
This struggle for existence, combined with variation, results in natural selection: the 'preservation of favourable variations and the rejection of injurious variations'. Those individuals that lose in the struggle for existence do not get to produce the next generation; those that win get to pass on their winning traits to their progeny. This means that the conditions of nature are constantly acting on individual variation, *automatically* rejecting the less improved forms of life (eventually leading to extinction) and preserving the perfected ones. If a single species is divided into two populations, natural selection will act on each population separately until each has accumulated enough differences to become a separate and new species.

And that was it. In these first four chapters – only a hundred pages or so in total – can be found the whole of Darwin's theory of evolution by natural selection. Because he was a scientist however, he went on to add a further ten chapters, going into enormous detail on matters such as 'Laws of Variation' and 'Hybridism', but in these four chapters alone lie all of his theory. In short, no species is immune from change; all have evolved – and are continuing to evolve – over many eons of time.

Darwin's scientific colleagues were generally won over to his theory within ten years. It immediately influenced many other scientists, such as the German biologist Ernst Haeckel (1834-

1919) who wrote *Evolution of Man* (1874) and sought to develop it further. No one has yet demolished it and, as paleontologists have continued filling in the gaps in the fossil record (which Darwin acknowledged was a difficulty for his theory at the time), it stands today as the most widely accepted and plausible mechanism for the fact of evolution.

It would seem that God did not, after all, engage in separate and innumerable acts of creation as the Bible suggests, and if the Bible was wrong about that, what else could it be wrong about? Such was the storm of controversy that the book evoked when it was first published, and it initiated a revolution in scientific and religious thought that continues to this day. Creationists, especially in the United States, continue to claim that Darwin was wrong, that evolution itself is still 'a theory' and cannot be proven, and we shall return to this contest in Week One of the course.

The Origin of Species appeared in six editions during Darwin's own lifetime. In the second edition (which followed in a matter of months because the first had sold out so quickly) he wrote: "I see no good reason why the views given in this volume should shock the religious feelings of any one." He had not written it atheistically, and he had no intention of promoting an atheistic mindset; he believed it was entirely possible for anyone to accept both God and evolution, just as he himself did, and he insisted that his work had nothing to do with the origin of life itself. Darwinian evolution did not preclude the existence of God.

The years following the publication of *The Origin of Species*, punctuated by serious and prolonged bouts of ill-health, were largely spent writing. He published three more major works, including *The Descent of Man* (1871), and began to write an autobiographical memoir that was not published in full until 1958. He died on 19 April 1882 at the age of 73 and was buried in Westminster Abbey.

Chapter Three

The Course

Week One: Led by the Spirit

Jesus, full of the Holy Spirit, returned from the Jordan and was led by the Spirit in the wilderness, where for forty days he was tempted by the devil. He ate nothing at all during those days, and when they were over, he was famished. (Luke 4.1-2)

Prelude

The Spirit who led Jesus into the wilderness after his baptism and before the start of his public ministry is the same Spirit who 'swept over the face of the waters' before Creation began (Genesis 1.2). The Greek word is *pneuma* and the Hebrew word *ruah*, a word of feminine gender meaning 'air', 'wind', or 'breath'. She is the breath of life that God breathed into the nostrils of a man (in Hebrew *adam*) who was formed from the dust of the ground (*adamah*) in Eden (Genesis 2.7); she is the Spirit who Jesus breathed on the disciples on the evening of the first Easter (John 20.22); she is the blast of wind who came crashing into the house in Jerusalem where the disciples were on the day of Pentecost (Acts 2.2).

In the Old Testament, the Spirit is closely identified with Wisdom (*Sofia*), who existed with God before the world began and who delighted in his work:

The LORD created me at the beginning of his work, the first of his acts of long ago. Ages ago I was set up, at the first, before the beginning of the earth. When there were no depths I was brought forth, when there were no springs abounding with water. Before the mountains had been shaped, before the hills, I was brought forth – when he had not yet made earth and fields, or the world's first bits of soil. (Proverbs 8.22-26)

The creation of the universe

'Then God said, "Let there be light"; and there was light' (Genesis 1.3). In July 2010 the European Space Agency's Planck observatory released an image of the first light to pass through the universe; it shows 'cosmic microwave background' radiation emitted 13.7 billion years ago. This radiation, the oldest light in the universe, was released about 400,000 years after the Big Bang – the unimaginably rapid expansion of concentrated energy at a single point in space and time – at the moment when the universe had cooled just enough for atoms to form and light to pass through it. It is the 'afterglow' of the Big Bang that created the universe.

Within this universe the earth is a small blue planet in a sun system at the edge of a galaxy of stars called the Milky Way. Astronomers estimate the total number of stars in the universe to be 300 sextillion (300,000 billion billion), with possibly trillions of earths orbiting them. Modern science tells us that planet earth has existed for billions of years (radiometric geology dates the oldest rocks on earth to an age of 4.5 billion years), and it is reckoned that the earth will sustain life for another five billion years before it becomes uninhabitable; this will occur when the sun turns into a red giant star, incinerating all life on earth, before collapsing into a tiny white dwarf star. As Keith Ward, Regius Professor of Divinity at Oxford University observes:

It will be an event of hardly any significance to the universe as a whole, which will go on existing for billions of years, perhaps evolving many forms of life more advanced than the human, for all we know... Human life seems very small in relation to the whole universe. (Ward 1998:20)

Nevertheless, human life is – for now at least – the most advanced form of life in the whole known universe. As Stephen Hawking and Leonard Mlodinow have written, "Although we are puny and insignificant on the scale of the cosmos, this makes us in a sense the lords of creation" (Hawking and Mlodinow 2010:9).

Until the sixteenth century, it was believed that the earth was at the centre of the universe; God lived in 'the heavens', quite literally in the sky above the earth. The Polish astronomer Copernicus (1473-1543) cast doubt on the geocentric myth when he put forward the idea that the earth and other planets orbit about the sun. The Italian astronomer and physicist Galileo (1564-1642) agreed with him, although in 1633 he was forced by the Inquisition of the Roman Catholic Church to recant. But the modern scientific viewpoint does nothing to diminish the grandeur of God – in fact God's sublimity, splendour, and magnificence are actually increased by the discoveries of science. Copernicus and Galileo enhanced God's domain, in much the same way that Darwin saw a greater and grander vision of God in the One who was capable of causing improvement of form in living organisms so that creatures could adapt and survive.

The creation of life

The source of life is the 'mystery of all mysteries'. Our own origins and our human place in the entire created order are things about which we seek to find answers. We can begin to find answers, I think, if we begin to understand that the process of the universe is the continual expression of the creative will of God; its actual existence needs to be attributed to the generosity of the Creator's love, for in the act of Creation God made room for something other than himself.

Professor Ward suggests that human beings could well be the reason why the whole universe was created. Physicists have calculated that the time it would take for complex life forms to evolve from basic atomic structures, in accordance with the basic laws of physics, would be in the order of ten to fifteen billion years. In other words, the universe needs to be the vast age and size it actually is for human beings to have evolved in accordance with the basic laws of physics. And if it was the Creator's desire to produce sentient beings who can come to understand the universe, to know the Creator and enter into a relationship of love with the Creator and his creation, then everything that exists in the whole universe will exist as part of a process whose goal is the existence of human beings who can share in the activity of God. Human life may, in the end, be what gives meaning and significance to the whole cosmic process.

So when did life begin? The fossil record, despite its incompleteness, tells us that unicellular plant life emerged on earth more than 3 billion years ago and multicellular animal life some 700 million years ago. Fossils are laid down in a pattern that serves as an index to living history, and the sequence of major groups of organisms appearing over geological time can be seen in the following table:

Fossil age (years)	Geological period	Organisms
Over 3 billion	Proterozoic	Plant cells without nuclei (like modern bacteria and algae)
1.5 billion	Proterozoic	Cells with nuclei (containing genetic information)
700 million	Ediacaran	The first multicellular animals

550 million	Cambrian	Corals and shellfish
480 million	Ordovician	Fish
380 million	Devonian	Amphibians and insects
340 million	Carboniferous	Reptiles
260 million	Permian	Dinosaurs
210 million	Triassic	Mammals
155 million	Jurassic	Birds

The picture we have is of life emerging from the water onto dry land and then taking to the air. The dinosaurs, successors to one reptilian line, became extinct in the Cretaceous period 65 million years ago following an asteroid impact. Their disappearance opened the evolutionary door to the mammals that survived the impact. With no dinosaurs eating all the vegetation, mammals were able to emerge from their shadow and grow spectacularly in size and diversity.

The evolutionary divergence of our human ancestors from the great apes began on the African continent more than 5 million years ago. The first member of the species *Homo sapiens* is recognized from around 150,000 years ago.

The creationist response
The response of creationism and the 'creation science' movement to all of this moves broadly in three directions:

1) Some creationists, who include the followers of Phillip

Johnson, a law professor at Berkeley University in California and author of *Darwin on Trial* (1991), choose to focus on the incompleteness of the fossil record, and seek to suggest that with all its gaps and imperfections, it represents nothing more than a deception. In so doing they attempt to discredit the physical evidence that forms the historical record of evolutionary change. It is quite true that the fossil record is incomplete, but paleontologists are continually filling in the gaps. The fact that particular fossil evidence has not yet been found does not, of course, mean that it does not exist, and because we have no further room to discuss the matter here I leave it to you to decide for yourself where you stand on this point.

2) Others, who include the followers of Henry Morris, founder of the Institute for Creation Research in California and author of *Scientific Creationism* (1974), choose to believe that the earth is less than 10,000 years old – because that is what the Bible says. By defending the chronology described in a literal reading of the Bible, these 'young-earth creationists' seek to invalidate the entire evidence for evolution: it could never have occurred for the simple reason that it never had time to occur. The apparent evolutionary sequences contained in the fossil record were all caused accidentally, they say, by Noah's Flood. Whether a literal reading of the Bible is appropriate in the context of this discussion is something we shall return to in Week Two.

3) Others, who include the followers of Michael Behe, a biochemistry professor at Lehigh University in Pennsylvania and author of *Darwin's Black Box* (1996), accept the fact of evolution – right down to the common ancestry of humans and the great apes. What they argue, however, is that this process of change cannot be the result of natural laws alone as instruments of God's plan and purpose, and claim that a 'designer' is required

to account for the complexity of life. They are the advocates of 'intelligent design' (ID), which we must explore briefly now before we begin the first group session.

In 1987, the creation science movement in the USA was dealt a severe blow when the US Supreme Court ruled that creationism was inherently religious rather than scientific and accordingly, should not be taught as part of the science curriculum in schools. As a result, some schools simply resorted to placing stickers on the inside of science textbooks warning readers that evolution is 'just a theory and not a fact'. In the aftermath of this ruling, ID became a strategy to enable the continued teaching of creation science in schools, presenting itself with scientific rather than religious credentials. In 2004, the Board of Dover High School in Pennsylvania voted to add ID to the school biology curriculum and drafted a statement on ID to be read to students. When Dover's biology teachers refused to comply the Board sent other employees into the classroom to read the statement instead. As a result, eleven parents filed a First Amendment lawsuit against the Board and the case went to trial in 2005. The judge's decision demolished the scientific pretensions of ID and declared it to be inherently religious.

It might appear from this strange episode that ID was a new scientific idea, a brand-new challenge to evolution, but it is actually a very old religious idea. One of its greatest advocates was the Reverend William Paley who we encountered in Chapter Two and shall meet again in Week Three of the course. It was an argument that Darwin himself considered and rejected in *The Origin of Species*. Paley used the metaphor of a watch and the watchmaker to explain the complexity of living organisms: the intricate workings of a watch do not simply come together by purposeless chance; the watch had a maker who had designed it for the purpose which it served, just like every organ of every living creature. Lamarck accepted design, as did some of

Darwin's closest allies (Asa Gray and Charles Lyell) who argued that the process of evolution was actively guided by God and led along certain beneficial lines. But Darwin could not accept this. In a letter to Gray in 1860 he wrote:

> I cannot see, as plainly as others do, & as I should wish to do, evidence of design & beneficence on all sides of us. There seems to me too much misery in the world. I cannot persuade myself that a beneficent & omnipotent God would have designedly created the Ichneumonidae with the express intention of their feeding within the living bodies of caterpillars, or that a cat should play with mice. (Darwin Correspondence Project www.darwinproject.ac.uk/entry-2814)

Any such designer looks not so much like God as an interfering meddler. He seems to be clever enough to design an African savanna elephant but not so clever that he can do it in one go, having to create and destroy many prototypes in the process. But it wasn't only the question of suffering that was a problem for Darwin, because the natural process of evolution also entailed much pain; he believed that if natural selection needed to be guided step by step, change by change, by an intelligent power, it effectively undid the whole of his theory. Divine guidance simply wasn't necessary for natural selection to operate, and rejecting it did not entail rejecting God. God ordinarily works in natural ways and by natural means, not supernatural ones.

Group Session

0.00 Leader

Welcome the group, introduce yourself, and run through any housekeeping points. Check that everyone has a copy of this book. Ask each member to say a few words about themselves – their name, where they live, what they do, and what their particular ministry is in their local church (e.g. mowing the churchyard, children's leader, sacristan, or baking cakes for church fundraising events). Check that each member of the group has read, and agrees to, the 'Rules of Engagement'. **10 minutes**

0.10 Film Clip 1
Darwin tells Annie about his encounter with an orangutan named 'Jenny' at London Zoo in 1838. **5 minutes**

0.15 Brainstorm
What did you find interesting or thought-provoking in that clip? What issues or questions does it raise for you? What would you like to come back to later if there is time? **5 minutes**

0.20 Group Discussion
Do you have any difficulties accommodating evolution with Christianity? Do you have any problems accepting Darwin's theory of natural selection as a plausible mechanism for species evolution? How do you feel about sharing a common ancestry with the anthropoid apes – the chimpanzee, gibbon, gorilla, and orangutan? **10 minutes**

0.30 In Small Groups
Talk about 'intelligent design'. What do you think of Paley's metaphor of a watch and the watchmaker? Do you believe that God has guided evolution, or do you think that natural processes alone (as distinct from supernatural ones) are sufficient for God's plan and purpose? What problems are inherent in a belief in ID? **10 minutes**

0.40 Feedback and Share
Leader: allow each small group to feedback and share with everyone else some of the things they have talked about. **5**

minutes

0.45 Film Clip 2

Joseph Hooker (a botanist and director of the Royal Botanic Gardens in Kew) and Thomas Huxley (a zoologist and ardent proponent of evolution popularly known as 'Darwin's bulldog') arrive at Down House in 1858 on a mission to persuade Darwin to publish his theory. **5 minutes**

0.50 Brainstorm

What did you find interesting or thought-provoking in that clip? What issues or questions does it raise for you? What would you like to come back to later if there is time? **5 minutes**

0.55 Group Discussion

Do you think Huxley is correct in telling Darwin 'You have killed God'? Evolution might prove some passages of scripture to be scientifically inaccurate, but does it make God 'an utterly redundant Almighty'? Where and how can you see God at work in the process of evolution? **10 minutes**

1.05 In Small Groups

Why do you think the Victorian Church found it so hard to accept evolution? Why do some Christians today still resist the evidence? What are the perceived problems it causes for the Church and her doctrine? (Try to think beyond the obvious fact that evolution is incompatible with some scriptural texts; we will be focusing on this next week). **10 minutes**

1.15 Feedback and Share

Leader: allow each small group to feedback and share with everyone else some of the things they have talked about. **5 minutes**

1.20 Meditation and Prayer

Reader 1

Then the LORD God formed man from the dust of the ground, and breathed into his nostrils the breath of life; and the man became a living being. (Genesis 2.7)

Pause

An extract from *The Origin of Species* (1st edition) by Charles Darwin:

> Analogy would lead me one step further, namely, to the belief that all animals and plants have descended from some one prototype... Therefore I should infer from analogy that probably all the organic beings which have ever lived on this earth have descended from some one primordial form, into which life was first breathed. (Darwin 1998:364)

Pause

An extract from *The Origin of Species* (2nd and subsequent editions):

> There is grandeur in this view of life, with its several powers, having been originally breathed by the Creator into a few forms or into one; and that, whilst this planet has gone cycling on according to the fixed law of gravity, from so simple a beginning endless forms most beautiful and most wonderful have been, and are being, evolved. (The Complete Works of Charles Darwin Online. www.darwin-online.org.uk)

One minute's silence for reflection
Reader 2

An extract from *Science and Creation* by the Reverend John Polkinghorne, Anglican priest and former Cambridge Professor of Mathematical Physics:

> Einstein once said, 'Religion without science is blind. Science without religion is lame.' His instinct that they need each other was right, though I would not describe their separate shortcomings in quite the terms he chose. Rather I would say, 'Religion without science is confined; it fails to be completely open to reality. Science without religion is incomplete; it fails to attain the deepest possible understanding.' The remarkable insights that science affords us into the intelligible workings of the world cry out for an explanation more profound than that which it itself can provide. Religion, if it is to take seriously its claim that the world is the creation of God, must be humble enough to learn from science what that world is actually like. The dialogue between them can only be mutually enriching. The scientist will find in theology a unifying principle more fundamental than the grandest unified field theory. The theologian will encounter in science's account of the pattern and structure of the physical world a reality which calls forth his admiration and wonder. Together they can say with the psalmist:
>
> O Lord how manifold are thy works!
> In wisdom thou hast made them all. (Psalm 104.24)
> (Polkinghorne 1988:97-98)

One minute's silence for reflection

Reader 3

An extract from *Finding Darwin's God* by Dr Kenneth Miller, Professor of Biology at Brown University, Rhode Island:

> The personal and physical presence of God in the Eden of Genesis was a source of comfort to those who sought to understand the complexity and the beauty of the living world, the diversity of which remained a mystery to even the most careful observer for most of human history.
>
> In the last two centuries, things have changed. Biology has developed from a purely descriptive science into a constructive one, and we now understand the genuine source of life's diversity. We have also lengthened our view to see that the story of life includes a grand, even heroic past, a record of change and struggle, of failure and triumph. As we add to the growing richness of life's documentary record, we can be justifiably proud, not just of the fact that we – along with every other living thing on the planet – are among life's winners, but especially of the fact that we are the very first creatures in 35 million centuries to become aware of the magnificence of our legacy.
>
> It is high time that we grew up and left the Garden. We are indeed Eden's children, yet it is time to place Genesis alongside the geocentric myth in the basket of stories that once, in a world of intellectual naivete, made helpful sense. As we walk through the gates, aware of the dazzling richness of the genuine biological world, there might even be a smile on the Creator's face – that at long last His creatures have learned enough to understand His world as it truly is. (Miller 2002:56. Copyright © 1999 by Kenneth R. Miller. Reprinted by permission of HarperCollins Publishers)

One minute's silence for reflection

Reader 4

Blessed are you, Lord God,
our light and our salvation;
to you be glory and praise for ever.
From the beginning you have created all things
and all your works echo the silent music of your praise.
In the fullness of time you made us in your image,
the crown of all creation.
You give us breath and speech, that with angels and
    archangels
and all the powers of heaven
we may find a voice to sing your praise:
Holy, holy, holy Lord,
God of power and might,
heaven and earth are full of your glory.
Hosanna in the highest.
(From Eucharistic Prayer G, Holy Communion Order One,
Common Worship: Services and Prayers for the Church of England)

Week Two: One Does Not Live by Bread Alone

The devil said to [Jesus], "If you are the Son of God, command this stone to become a loaf of bread." Jesus answered him, "It is written, 'One does not live by bread alone.'" (Luke 4.3-4)

Prelude

As we continue our Lenten journey, it is appropriate that we consider our Lord's temptations. As we ourselves engage in an intensive struggle with the enemies of the soul, nothing could be more inspiring than to consider how Jesus met and defeated those self-same forces at the outset of his ministry. If Jesus had not been tempted, we would not be able to say with any conviction that he was fully human.

His first temptation arose out of his own physical needs – 'he was famished'. The temptation was for Jesus to exercise his divine ability, abusing his position of power by serving his own needs rather than depending on God's provision for his needs. Human life is defined here as being about trusting in God and not about meeting our own needs. The work of the Son of God (and of us, even in our own desert experiences) will have to involve more than that.

In Matthew's gospel we get a slightly different version of the saying: Matthew adds to the last sentence, '...but by every word that comes from the mouth of God'. Given that Jesus is quoting Deuteronomy 8.3, it seems that Matthew's account is more precise, and we are left wondering why Luke chose to truncate the saying. You will have some time to discuss this at the beginning of the group session, and what we need to think about now is 'the word of God'.

The Holy Bible

The Bible (excluding the Apocrypha) is a 'library' of 66 books – history, law, poetry, biography, letters and more – 39 in the Old

Testament and 27 in the New Testament. They are not placed in chronological order of writing, and some of them were written by many different hands, revised and edited over many years before reaching the final version that has been passed down to us. Both the Old and New Testaments make up the Christian Bible.

The oldest parts of the Old Testament probably originated in around 1250 B.C. (about the time of the exodus from Egypt), yet they recount events, beliefs, and laws belonging to a period some eight centuries earlier. So behind the written word of the Bible lies the experience of more than two thousand years in which the Hebrew people and the first Christians were convinced that God was making himself known to them. They experienced this revelation within the context of their everyday lives and against the backcloth of the history of their time, so everything that was eventually written down (much of it from oral tradition) was framed within the culture – the social, moral, intellectual, and religious structures – of a time and place very different from our own.

Because the origins of the Bible are so steeped in history and culture, it means that today we have to wrestle with scripture and 'inculturate' its message – to interpret and translate it into contemporary forms, to spell it out in clear and meaningful ways that have relevance to the people of our time and place. This 'cross-cultural interpretation' is important because if the Church is preaching a message that sounds and feels as if it belongs to history, then the exercise is a futile one and the Church will fail in her mission.

Genesis 1 was never meant to be a scientific or factual account of the creation of the cosmos. It was written late in the history of the Jewish people, perhaps at the time of their exile in Babylon (597-539 B.C.), and it serves as a pre-scientific reflection on the one true God (among many gods) who had freed their ancestors from slavery in Egypt, formed them into his holy nation, and would now free them again from bondage in another foreign land. The God who had created the whole universe, who had power above all the pagan gods of Babylon, would certainly be able to do this! The creation myth reassured the exiles of their place in the grand scheme of things, and produced a sense of unity and purpose among them.

Because the Bible was written by human beings, it cannot be untouched by human experience. Yet through divine inspiration, these men and women were enabled to speak words that are able to convey the truth of God. 'All scripture is inspired by God', Paul wrote in his Second Letter to Timothy (2 Timothy 3.16), 'God-breathed' being a more literal rendering of the word translated 'inspired'. And in Peter's words, 'Men and women moved by the Holy Spirit spoke from God' (2 Peter 1.21). So the Holy Spirit inspired the human authors but did not dictate what they wrote. As such we could say that whilst scripture *derives* its authority from God, it is the Church that *bestows* authority upon it; the authority of the Bible is not located in the book itself but in the Church's recognition of the importance of what it contains.

For Christians, the Bible occupies a place of supreme authority as a foundation for our knowledge of God, because Jesus Christ is known to us primarily through scripture. But scripture is the testimony to this main revelation, Jesus 'the Word' (John 1.1), rather than the revelation itself, and so the emphasis falls on the One to whom scripture bears witness rather than on the text of scripture itself. Christ is the Word of God in the primary sense, and the Bible, which points beyond itself to the Word of God, is only the word of God in a secondary sense. Christ cannot be reduced to a text and requires interpretation through human experience which is why the four Gospels each make Christ known in different ways: they reflect the concerns of the Christian communities for whom they were written at the time they were written, and each represents a different cultural interpretation of the original gospel message.

We can perhaps gain a clearer understanding of all of this if we compare it to Muslim attitudes concerning their sacred text, the Qur'an, as a mode of divine revelation.

The Holy Qur'an

In the great religion of Islam, the Qur'an is the word of God revealed to the Prophet Muhammad (born in Mecca c. 570 A.D.) via the archangel Gabriel. When Muslims affirm that Muhammad is God's prophet, they are saying that his revelations really are the authentic voice of God. Muhammad's first revelation of the Qur'an came to him in the Cave of Hira outside Mecca in 610. The revelations continued over a period of 22 years, in Mecca and later in Medina following the migration of the Prophet and his followers there in 622 due to hostility against them in Mecca. Muhammad recited every addition to his followers and they were recorded by pious scribes. By the time of the Prophet's death in 632, the entire Qur'an had been written down and after his death these writings were gathered into a single book.

Whilst Muslims have different traditions of interpretation of the Qur'an (Sunni, Shi'a and Sufi) they nevertheless hold that it is the very word or speech of God. It remains unchanged and preserved to this day in its original form; it is uncorrupted and undistorted; no human words have been added to the divine words. Classic Islamic teaching maintains the divine origins, inerrancy, and infallibility of the Qur'an, a position we call 'fundamentalism'.

Interestingly, the term 'fundamentalism' was a designation originally applied to an element of Christian orthodoxy: Biblical fundamentalism emerged as a conservative movement within Protestantism in the USA in the late nineteenth century, teaching the literal truth of the Bible and its wholly divine origins in direct response to Darwinism and other scientific discovery. Some of today's creationists are continuing these dogmas in their insistence that Creation took place in accordance with the accounts given in the Old Testament.

One of the problems with Biblical fundamentalism is that it seems to invite criticism of religion from people like Richard Dawkins, a prominent evolutionary biologist from Oxford University. Dawkins, who is an atheist, is presumably against religion *per se*, but his assaults appear to be mounted principally against creationism and the creation science movement – the 'soft underbelly' of religion. For example, his 1986 book *The Blind Watchmaker*, a criticism of intelligent design (with a title referencing to Paley's metaphor), is presented as if ID is a current idea and one that is widely-subscribed to today by God's faithful people. I would say it is not, and if Professor Dawkins really wants to convince me that my faith in God is misplaced, he needs to come up with something better than this.

The bigger problem, though, with Biblical fundamentalism is that it seems to ignore *reason*, and this is the final issue we must think about before we begin the next group session.

Scripture, tradition and reason
Faith is the gift of God to his people – a faith grounded in both scripture and the traditions of the Church (for example our creeds and confessions of faith, and the teaching of the Church Fathers and the ecumenical Councils). And so also is reason – the power to think, understand, and form judgements logically. Faith and reason are both gifts from God and to accept only faith and reject reason would seem to be a profound misuse of God's gifts. The use of our God-given intellect is a way in which we can come to know something about the nature, character, and purposes of God, and so allow us to participate in the activity of God. This, as we explored last week, might just be the reason why God created life in the first place.

Anglicans like me are not, as a rule, creationists. This is because Richard Hooker (1554-1600), one of the first theologians of the English Reformation and one who did more than any other to clarify the intellectual bases of Anglicanism, taught us long ago to hold scripture, tradition, and reason in a dynamic relationship with each other. This is the 'three-legged stool' of Anglicanism; if you remove any one of these three legs then Anglicanism will fall over!

Anglicanism sought to find a 'middle way' between the extremes of Puritanism on the one hand (which was extremely faithful to scripture) and Catholicism on the other (which was extremely faithful to tradition). It also gave space for reason – though this was not a new idea but one established at the time of the Renaissance. In essence what we ought to be doing is testing scripture against reason, reason against tradition, and tradition against scripture. Let me give you some examples:

1) *Testing scripture against reason.* The creation narratives are obviously a good example of this process: everything I know about their origins, as well as the modern scientific worldview, suggests to me that these particular passages of scripture should not be interpreted literally or relied upon as an authoritative description of how the world began. In this example, scripture has failed the test of reason: reason wins over scripture. (If you want to listen to an opposing view, the *Creation* DVD contains an interview with a young-earth creationist, Professor Andy McIntosh; select 'Special Features' from the main menu then go to 'Darwin's Legacy').

2) *Testing reason against tradition.* I confess this to you with some hesitancy, but I have always been a bit unsure about the virgin birth. It's not that I don't believe in miracles, because I do, but there are two reasons for my uncertainty. The first is that I want to believe that Jesus was fully human; to deny this is to be guilty of the Docetist heresy (Docetism held that Christ only *appeared* to be human and consequently he only *appeared* to suffer), and reason tells me that human beings cannot be born to virgins (except by modern methods like IVF). There is

also the matter of Jesus' Y-chromosome to account for, which is only present in males and can only be passed from father to son. Secondly, I have always wondered why Paul, Mark and John appear to have known nothing about the virgin birth. At least they never mention it in their writings, and this has done nothing to lessen their conviction that Jesus is the Son of God. The accounts of the virgin birth in Matthew and Luke don't seem to add anything to the true meaning of the Christian story – that 'the Word became flesh and lived among us' (John 1.14). If anything, they seem to detract from this message by suggesting that that 'flesh' was not really flesh at all, and that Jesus' human ancestry cannot actually be traced back through Joseph to King David as the New Testament elsewhere wants us to believe (e.g. Romans 1.3, 2 Timothy 2.8). Nevertheless, the virgin birth is such an important part of the tradition of the Church – for instance I am called to affirm my belief in it every time I say the Creed – I am prepared to believe it as a matter of faith. In this example, reason has failed the test of tradition: tradition wins over reason.

3) *Testing tradition against scripture.* In the medieval western Church a tradition emerged about a place called Purgatory. This was a third place between the stark alternatives of heaven and hell, where certain sinners might be saved from hell by some kind of purging or washing process in a cleansing fire and so be made ready to enter the joy of heaven. The length of time they spent in Purgatory could be alleviated by the prayers of the living. The Reformers opposed the doctrine of purgatory because, in their view, it was based on flimsy Biblical evidence, and Purgatory was consigned to the history books. In this example, tradition has failed the test of scripture: scripture wins over tradition.

Group Session

0.00 Bible Study
Compare Luke 4.4 with Matthew 4.4 and Deuteronomy 8.3. What point is Matthew making? Why do you think Luke chose to truncate the saying – is he trying to make a different point?

We all know what it's like to be tempted and to hear the voice of the tempter (or temptress) whispering in our ear. It is a universal human experience – and of course it's not wrong to be tempted, it is giving in to temptation that we have to try to resist. How does the devil try to win one over you? (Try not to trivialize temptation and make it only about chocolate and cream cakes). **10 minutes**

0.10 Film Clip 1
Darwin's devoutly Christian wife, Emma, confronts him over his apparent unbelief. **5 minutes**

0.15 Brainstorm
What did you find interesting or thought-provoking in that clip? What issues or questions does it raise for you? What would you like to come back to later if there is time? **5 minutes**

0.20 Group Discussion
Emma tells Darwin: 'I think that you are at war with God'. Darwin might not agree; his 'war' is principally with the Biblical account of the origin of species (though he is also grappling with the problem of suffering). What other passages of scripture do you find hard to believe because they fail the test of reason? Does your reasoning pass the test of tradition? Can you think of any traditions that fail the test of scripture? **10 minutes**

0.30 In Small Groups
Is it possible to believe the creation narratives in *both* Genesis 1

and Genesis 2? Think about the accounts of Creation and Fall in Genesis 1-3: to what extent do you think these narratives can be read figuratively rather than literally? What is in these stories that you particularly like which – even if not a literal truth – still imparts some important meaning to life? (For example, I really like this as an observation on Genesis 2.21-23: woman was not created from man's head to be above him; nor was she created from his feet to be trampled on by him; she was taken from his side to be equal to him, from under his arm to be held by him, and from near his heart to be loved by him). **10 minutes**

0.40 Feedback and Share
Leader: allow each small group to feedback and share with everyone else some of the things they have talked about. **5 minutes**

0.45 Film Clip 2
Darwin goes to church and doesn't like what he hears. **5 minutes**

0.50 Brainstorm
What did you find interesting or thought-provoking in that clip? What issues or questions does it raise for you? What would you like to come back to later if there is time? **5 minutes**

0.55 Group Discussion
The Reverend John Brodie Innes, vicar of Downe, tells his congregation that suffering is for our own good, 'the corrections of a wise and affectionate parent'. Do you agree? He also says: 'even a sparrow falls not to the ground without [God's] will'. Innes is misinterpreting Matthew 10.29. In its proper context (verses 26-31, beginning and ending with the command 'do not be afraid'), what is Jesus actually saying? (It may be helpful to look also at 6.26). How has Innes twisted this to make a very different and unhelpful point? **10 minutes**

1.05 In Small Groups

Having already thought about some passages of scripture you *can't* believe because they defy reason, are there any you don't *want* to believe because you think 'that is not what God is like'? Is it okay to reject them? Imagine that you have been asked to read Exodus 12.29-30 in church on Sunday and, at the end, you are expected to say, 'This is the word of the Lord'. How do you feel about that? **10 minutes**

1.15 Feedback and Share

Leader: allow each small group to feedback and share with everyone else some of the things they have talked about. **5 minutes**

1.20 Meditation and Prayer

Reader 1

In the beginning was the Word, and the Word was with God, and the Word was God. He was in the beginning with God. All things came into being through him, and without him not one thing came into being. What has come into being in him was life, and the life was the light of all people. The light shines in the darkness, and the darkness did not overcome it. (John 1.1-5)

Pause

We declare to you what was from the beginning, what we have heard, what we have seen with our eyes, what we have looked at and touched with our hands, concerning the word of life – this life was revealed, and we have seen it and testify to it, and declare to you the eternal life that was with the Father and was revealed to us. (1 John 1.1-2)

Pause

Long ago God spoke to our ancestors in many and various ways by the prophets, but in these last days he has spoken to us by a Son, whom he appointed heir of all things, through whom he also created the worlds. He is the reflection of God's glory and the exact imprint of God's very being, and he sustains all things by his powerful word. (Hebrews 1.1-3)

One minute's silence for reflection

Reader 2

An extract from *Faith Thinking* by Dr Trevor Hart, University of Aberdeen:

A genuinely critical Christian theology, I have argued, will be firmly rooted in the tradition of faith, while open to the inevitable and necessary reformation of that tradition through critical reflection and interaction with new sources of knowledge, new ways of seeing things. The story must be retold for a new human audience. The message must be translated into a new intellectual and cultural language. The living Word must become incarnate again...

This means that theologians must frequently make difficult judgements in pursuit of a coherent and integrated story to tell. When should the tradition be reformed and recast in accordance with new insights and learning; and when should it be allowed to exercise a caustic and potentially transformative role, standing out from the crowd and offering an alternative way of seeing things? When should we be flexible, bending with the winds of change? And on what issues should we stand firm, purveyors of salt and light to a society ridden with darkness and decay? The issue at stake here is that of continuity with the apostolic tradition. How much change is legitimate and necessary to the task of translating the message? And when does it mutate into another message altogether? Knowing which ditches to die in, identifying the 'enduring impurities' which must be held on to and rendered in meaningful terms for every new context, these are the judgements which face those engaged in fashioning a critical and contemporary Christian theology. (Hart 1995:219-220)

One minute's silence for reflection

Reader 3

An extract from *The Orthodox Way* by Bishop Kallistos Ware, Orthodox Eastern Church:

What is the attitude of the Orthodox Church towards the critical study of the Bible as it has been carried on in the West over the past two centuries? Since our reasoning brain is a gift from God, there is undoubtedly a legitimate place for scholarly research into Biblical origins. But, while we are not to reject this research wholesale, we cannot as Orthodox accept it in its entirety. Always we need to keep in view that the Bible is not just a collection of historical documents, but it is *the book of the Church, containing God's word...*

As we read the Bible, we are all the time gathering information, wrestling with the sense of obscure sentences, comparing and analyzing. But this is secondary. The real purpose of Bible study is much more than this – to feed our love for Christ, to kindle our hearts into prayer, and to provide us with guidance in our personal life. The study of words should give place to an immediate dialogue with the living Word himself. "Whenever you read the Gospel," says St Tikhon of Zadonsk, "Christ himself is speaking to you. And while you read, you are praying and talking with him"...

Approached in a prayerful manner, the Bible is found to be always contemporary – not just writings composed in the distant past but a message addressed directly to me here and now. (Ware 1995:110-111)

One minute's silence for reflection

Reader 4

Come, my Light, and illuminate my darkness.
Come, my Life, and revive me from death.
Come, my Physician, and heal my wounds.
Come, Flame of divine love, and burn up the thorns of my sins,
kindling my heart with the flame of thy love.
Come, my King, sit upon the throne of my heart and reign there.
For thou alone art my King and my Lord.
(St Dimitrii of Rostov, seventeenth-century Russian Orthodox bishop)

Week Three: Worship the Lord your God
and Serve Only Him

Then the devil led [Jesus] up and showed him in an instant all the kingdoms of the world. And the devil said to him, "To you I will give their glory and all this authority; for it has been given over to me, and I give it to anyone I please. If you, then, will worship me, it will all be yours." Jesus answered him, "It is written, 'Worship the Lord your God, and serve only him.' " (Luke 4.5-8)

Prelude

Jesus' second temptation was to an unworthy compromise: 'If you worship me, all the kingdoms of the world will be yours'. Now, not all compromise is bad – without it I don't think that two people would ever be able to live together! But here the suggested compromise is an evil one – to recognize the supremacy of the devil, to worship and serve him. It is said that 'every person has their price'. We are reminded of the legend of Faust, who surrendered his soul to the devil in return for youth, knowledge, and magical power. We can think of Edmund in *The Lion, the Witch and the Wardrobe* (C. S. Lewis, 1950) who surrendered his soul to the White Witch for some more Turkish Delight. Jesus replies, 'It is written – worship the Lord your God and serve only him'. Any pursuit, priority, or preoccupation that diverts us from that purpose should be seen for what it is: the devil's temptation.

It strikes me that creation science is a kind of compromise – not an evil one, of course, but not a very good one either. It tries to be *both* religion *and* science, and ends up being neither authentically. We saw in Chapter Two how intrinsically linked were the disciplines of science and religion in the nineteenth century: science was an amateur pastime of the wealthy and educated clergy, many of whom found time to combine scientific study with their clerical duties, and Darwin himself might well have become one of them. The scientific establishment – the Royal Society itself – was populated by deeply devout men who sought to better their understanding of God through the study of science. Scientific investigation was regarded as an excellent way of getting closer to the Creator. Science was almost a branch of theology, and it was this fusion of science with religion that led to the flourishing of 'natural theology', the search for knowledge of God through the exercise of reason and the inspection of the world.

Church and science in the Victorian era

In St. Paul's letter to the Romans he wrote: "Ever since the creation of the world [God's] eternal power and divine nature, invisible though they are, have been understood and seen through the things he has made" (Romans 1.20). The natural world acts as a window into the character and purposes of God; the God who made the world can be known through the world that he created. However, it was not until the Middle Ages that natural theology really took hold in Christian thought, notably at the hands of St. Anselm (1033-1109). The scientific rebirth of the Renaissance furthered its popularity, its great appeal lying in a search for understanding. It was this same search for understanding that led to a second resurgence or revival of natural theology in England in the late eighteenth and early nineteenth centuries against the backdrop of the Industrial Revolution, when its leading figures were the Reverend William Paley, Archdeacon of Carlyle, and the Reverend John Bird Sumner (who later became Archbishop of Canterbury 1848-62).

At Cambridge University, Darwin read Paley's *View of the Evidences of Christianity* (1794) and *Natural Theology* (1802). He had also read Sumner's *The Evidence of Christianity derived from its Nature and Reception* (1821), and both authors impressed him. This is Paley on 'The Goodness of the Deity' from *Natural Theology*:

The parts, therefore, especially the limbs and senses of animals, although they constitute, in mass and quantity, a small portion of the material creation, yet, since they alone are instruments of perception, they compose what may be called the whole of visible nature, estimated with a view to the disposition of its author. Consequently, it is in *these* that we are to seek his character. It is by these that we are to prove that the world was made with a benevolent design.

Nor is the design abortive. It is a happy world, after all. The air, the earth, the water, teem with delighted existence. In a spring noon, or a summer evening, on whichever side I turn my eyes, myriads of happy beings crowd upon my view. (http://books.google.com)

The key word here, perhaps, is 'prove'. Paley's 'Evidences' and Sumner's 'Evidence' appealed to Darwin's own delight in rational thought, in reasoning, logic, and scientific evidence, but the problem with natural theology – 'this so-called science' as John Henry Newman referred to it – was that it had little to do with Jesus Christ and even less with the activity of the Holy Spirit. Newman said of it: "It cannot be Christian, in any true sense, at all", nor can it "tell us one word about Christianity proper". Christianity had become a series of hypotheses to be established and arguments to be won, rather than an authentic experience of God. As Nick Spencer, Director of Studies at *Theos* observes:

Darwin's pre-*Beagle* Christianity was a synthesis of Paley and Sumner: dogmatic, ordered, disciplined, reasonable, civilized, benign. It had limited time for revelation and virtually none for personal experience. Christ was not so much a person to be transformed by as a theorem to be proved. God was less the ground of our being, to which the sense of the sublime served as testimony, as he was the conclusion of a logical argument. (Spencer 2009:15)

This was the faith that Darwin lost when tragedy struck at Easter 1851. Natural theology seemed to be blind to all the pain and suffering in the world, and gave him no resources for dealing with Annie's tragic death. As far as Darwin was concerned, Paley had failed 'to prove that the world was made with a benevolent design'. There were volcanoes and earthquakes, foxes ate rabbits, and children died. This did not disprove the existence of God, but it did make him question whether an unjust world of triumphant evil and endless suffering could possibly be grounded in, and guided by, a good and righteous God. What Darwin never went on to do was to look for where God *is* in all the suffering of his Creation. Had he done so, he would have discovered the crucified God, and he might have discovered also that whilst God may be known through nature, it is Jesus Christ who tells us what God is really like and who makes God known to the world.

Ironically, it was Darwin himself who dealt a mortal blow to the natural theology of his day. It was his theory of natural selection, with its emphasis on the struggle for existence in which all living things are engaged, which cast doubt on Paley's 'happy world of delighted existence', and it questioned Paley's most significant argument for the contrivance of a Designer. The old-style natural theology of Paley and Sumner is dead. So is the 'God of the Gaps', whose only role was to explain the scientifically inexplicable. God is to be found in what we know rather than in what we don't know. God wants us to be aware of his presence not in unsolved problems but in those that are solved. So it is that science and religion, rightfully separated, can still inform each other in a mutually enriching dialogue. This is a revisal rather than a revival of natural theology, and the modern creation science movement (which is religion masquerading as science) should be careful not to muddy the water.

Several recent scientific observations, such as the 'anthropic principle' (which says that human life would never have emerged had any one of the fundamental forces underpinning the universe – gravity, electromagnetism, and the nuclear forces – been different to even the minutest degree) and the 'deep structure' of evolution (the apparent tendency for evolution to 'find' the same pathway to a solution to many complex problems), have tempted a resurgence of the kind of natural theology from which Darwin emerged. The first observation suggests that the physical constants of the universe were 'set up' in a way that made our existence possible – a seemingly 'life-tailored' universe. The second observation suggests that evolution might have a purpose and direction after all. This may be encouraging for Christians, but Nick Spencer warns us:

> Darwin's story reminds us, forcefully, that to *base* religious faith on such observations is a serious mistake, inviting collapse when the next scientific revolution comes. It is one thing to investigate such phenomena as objectively as one can, and then to explore how consonant they are with a Christian understanding of creation. It is quite another to treat them as a foundation stone for one's faith. (Spencer 2009:117)

Science and religion occupy distinctly different domains, the material and the spiritual, and each must be allowed to follow its own direction. Science and religion answer different questions about the world, the 'how' and the 'why'. Each will inform the other and each will be found to offer its own pathway to God. Paul Davies, an Australian physicist, has even written: 'It may be bizarre but in my opinion science offers a surer road to God than religion' (Davies 1990:ix). That is interesting, but it should not turn all Christians into scientists or draw us back to the mindset of natural theology in the nineteenth century.

Church and education in the Victorian era
Just as religion and science were inherently entwined in the

nineteenth century, so were religion and education. Darwin's own education before the age of nine was at the Unitarian chapel and the parish church, and we have already seen from his time at Cambridge how the university system at the time was grounded in and governed by the Church – specifically the Church of England as the established church of the nation. (Newman, whose criticism of natural theology was mentioned earlier, had to resign as a Fellow of Oriel College, Oxford, the moment he converted to Rome in 1845). The influence of the Church in education pervaded the whole system, from the top universities to the smallest village schools. Outside the sphere of private schools, the Church *was* the educational system, and this is because the Church – in the absence of any state provision – had set it up.

In my current parish of Gillingham (hard 'G' as in Gilbert) in north Dorset, the following leaflet was distributed around the town in 1839:

GILLINGHAM

A National School for Girls and Boys will shortly be opened at the new School Room, near the Vicarage. All the children will be taught reading, writing, summing and knitting, and the girls will be taught needlework. Each child will pay one penny a week. No child can be admitted under six years old; nor any who does not know the alphabet. Parents wishing to send their children to this School are requested to call at the Vicarage any morning between eight and ten o'clock.

The tradition continues, one way or another, to the present day. It is most evident, of course, in the many Church Schools (primary and secondary) that flourish as an integral part of our state-maintained schools system. In the wider sphere, the 1988 Education Reform Act actually requires a daily 'act of collective worship' in all maintained schools, and stipulates that it should be 'wholly or mainly of a broadly Christian character'. Whether this happens or not is another matter, yet this law from as recently as 1988 stands in the statute book as testimony to the Church's important role in education down the ages.

By the early 1900s the Church was also taking education to the farthest corners of the British Empire – and the world beyond – as part of its missionary endeavour. Education meant secular schooling, not simply Christian education, and it was given on the assumption that the recipients would emerge as Christians. Christianity was regarded as a civilizing force that would have a beneficial moral impact on indigenous populations who did not yet know the love of Christ, but there was little understanding in those days of the importance of 'cross-cultural mission' – taking the gospel to people where and how they are, not where and how you would like them to be. Evangelization in the Victorian era was a process of introducing British values and culture (education, health, prosperity) to people of very different cultures; it involved imposing a 'white, western European Christianity' on people with whom that did not sit easily, and problems inevitably resulted.

The mission to the Fuegians
Part of *HMS Beagle's* task when she set sail from Plymouth in 1831 was to establish a Christian mission on the Tierra del Fuego archipelago. We are going to be seeing this in the group session, so it will be helpful to set the scene now.

On the *Beagle's* first voyage around South America – the one that Captain Fitzroy had completed after Captain Stokes shot himself – Fitzroy took three Fuegian children back to England with him with a view to having them educated and civilized.

This, of course, meant converting them to Christianity. His plan was that he would then take them back to Tierra del Fuego to found a mission settlement. The children were a girl called 'Fuegia Basket' and two boys, 'Jemmy (James) Button' and 'Hope Memory'. Hope Memory died of smallpox in England, but on the *Beagle's* subsequent voyage two years later – the one that Darwin went on – Fitzroy duly returned Fuegia Basket and Jemmy Button to their homeland, under the oversight of the Reverend Richard Matthews of the Church Mission Society. We will see what happened shortly!

Group Session

0.00 Bible Study
Where is Jesus quoting from? If someone in the group has an annotated Bible or 'Study Bible' you will be guided to this very quickly, which proves just how useful they are! Look up the text and read it in its context. What other 'gods' do people follow in the present age? The choices we face are not always 'black and white', and the temptations we experience not always clearly recognizable: can you think of any situations where you or someone you know has come to an unworthy compromise? **10 minutes**

0.10 Film Clip 1
Darwin tells Annie about the mission to the Fuegians. **5 minutes**

0.15 Brainstorm
What did you find interesting or thought-provoking in that clip? What issues or questions does it raise for you? What would you like to come back to later if there is time? **5 minutes**

0.20 Group Discussion
Do you agree that Christianity can be a civilizing force – that 'good Christian values can tame the most savage of hearts' and

that by their example the Fuegian children could 'bring their fellow savages to God'? Do you think that bringing education, health and prosperity to a people *in order that* they become Christians might be a perversion of missionary work? How has the missionary work of the Church changed since the nineteenth century and where do its focuses lie now? **10 minutes**

0.30 In Small Groups

Talk about the involvement of the Church in education in Britain today. What benefits do you think Church Schools bring to their pupils that other schools do not? What problems are associated with the requirement for all maintained schools to hold a daily 'act of collective worship wholly or mainly of a broadly Christian character'? Do you agree that other Faith Schools should be allowed to operate within the system alongside Church Schools? **10 minutes**

0.40 Feedback and Share

Leader: allow each small group to feedback and share with everyone else some of the things they have talked about. **5 minutes**

0.45 Film Clip 2

In 1858, before his own book is ready for publication, Darwin receives a letter from Alfred Russel Wallace outlining an identical evolutionary theory. **5 minutes**

0.50 Brainstorm

What did you find interesting or thought-provoking in that clip? What issues or questions does it raise for you? What would you like to come back to later if there is time? **5 minutes**

0.55 Group Discussion

Try to list all the things shown in this clip that are not good in

Darwin's life and in his observations on the world around him – does this look to you like Paley's 'happy world of delighted existence'? Innes' response to all of this is: 'The Lord moves in mysterious ways' and 'it is not for us to speculate on God's reasons'. Do you think these are appropriate responses to the problem of suffering? How would you respond to Darwin? **10 minutes**

1.05 In Small Groups

Talk about natural theology. How and why did science and religion become so entwined in the early nineteenth century? What advantages can you see today in the separation of science and religion, yet with a mutually enriching dialogue between them? Do you think that creation science appears to be some kind of compromise? **10 minutes**

1.15 Feedback and Share

Leader: allow each small group to feedback and share with everyone else some of the things they have talked about. **5 minutes**

1.20 Meditation and Prayer

Reader 1

[Christ] is the image of the invisible God, the firstborn of all creation; for in him all things in heaven and on earth were created, things visible and invisible, whether thrones or dominions or rulers or powers – all things have been created through him and for him. He himself is before all things, and in him all things hold together. He is the head of the body, the church; he is the beginning, the firstborn from the dead, so that he might come to have first place in everything. For in him all the fullness of God was pleased to dwell, and through him God was pleased to reconcile to himself all things, whether on earth or in heaven, by making peace through the blood of his cross. (Colossians 1.15-20)

Pause

No one has ever seen God. It is God the only Son, who is close to the Father's heart, who has made him known. (John 1.18)

Pause

God does not want to be known except through Christ; nor can he be known in any other way. (Martin Luther, 1535)

One minute's silence for reflection

Reader 2

An extract from *The Hardest Part* by the Reverend G. A. Studdert Kennedy, army chaplain in the First World War, affectionately known as 'Woodbine Willie':

When I had been in France as a chaplain about two months, before I had heard a gun fired or seen a trench, I went to see an officer in a base hospital who was slowly recovering from very serious wounds. The conversation turned on religion, and he seemed anxious to get at the truth. He asked me a tremendous question. "What I want to know, Padre," he said, "is, what is God like? I never thought much about it before this war. I took the world for granted. I was not religious, though I was confirmed and went to Communion some times with my wife. But now it all seems different. I realise that I am a member of the human race, and have a duty towards it, and that makes me want to know what God is like..."

When the question was put to me in hospital I pointed to a crucifix which hung over the officer's bed, and said, "Yes, I think I can tell you. God is like that." I wondered if it would satisfy him. It did not. He was silent for a while, looking at the crucifix, and then he turned to me, and his face was full of doubt and disappointment. "What do you mean?" he said; "God cannot be like that. God is Almighty, Maker of heaven and earth, Monarch of the world, the King of kings, the Lord of lords, Whose will sways all the world. That is a battered, wounded, bleeding figure, nailed to a cross and helpless, defeated by the world and broken in all but spirit. That is not God..." (Studdert Kennedy 2007:7-8)

One minute's silence for reflection

Reader 3

An extract from *Christianity Rediscovered* by Father Vincent Donovan, Roman Catholic missionary to the Masai:

At other times the will was there to override the weaknesses in the community, the will to ask the Spirit to come on this community to change it into the Body of Christ, so that we could say together, "This – not just the bread and wine, but the whole life of the village, its work, play, joy, sorrow, the homes, the grazing fields, the flocks, the people – all this is my Body."

The leaders made the decision, and asked me to say again the words of institution. And we took and ate. And we sent some of the blessed bread to the sick in bed. The singers liked the Our Father so much they sang it twice.

Some got up to go to bed. Many stayed on still

discussing several things. The singers finally began to tire and the singing dwindled. It was now after ten o'clock at night.

I stood up and said, "May God the Father, his son Jesus, and his Spirit bless you. Go and sleep in peace. In your homes tonight, in your work tomorrow, in your contact with other villages and other people, this Mass is continuing. It really does not end, does it? May your Mass never end. May your Mass be beautiful. Work well and for others. Your homes, your flocks, your children, your work with all these things – your life. *Ite, Missa Est*. Go to it. It is the Mass." (Donovan 1982:127-128)

One minute's silence for reflection

Reader 4

Almighty God,
we receive new life
from the supper your Son gave us in this world.
May we find full contentment
in the meal we hope to share
in your eternal kingdom.
(Prayer after Communion, Mass of the Lord's Supper on Holy Thursday, *The Sunday Missal*)

Week Four: Do Not Put the Lord your God to the Test

Then the devil took [Jesus] to Jerusalem, and placed him on the pinnacle of the temple, saying to him, "If you are the Son of God, throw yourself down from here, for it is written, 'He will command his angels concerning you, to protect you,' and 'On their hands they will bear you up, so that you will not dash your foot against a stone.' " Jesus answered him, "It is said, 'Do not put the Lord your God to the test.' " (Luke 4.9-12)

Prelude

The third and final temptation, occurring in Jerusalem, was to presumption and pride, which is almost the exact opposite of compromise. If Jesus had the promise of God's protection then why not draw on it by throwing himself off the pinnacle of the temple and surviving? Surely such a public demonstration of invincibility would help him win the support and assent of the people. So will Jesus presume upon God and put himself in a tight corner where God will have to intervene? Of course not; Jesus replies, 'It is said – do not put the Lord your God to the test'.

No person has the right to think they stand in so privileged a position with God that they can afford to neglect the laws of the universe and the realities of everyday life. It is not for us to test God; rather we must accept how the world works, live our lives and bear our burdens. The power of God will not always be displayed in lifting us out of the sufferings of the world, but in enabling us to live courageously in the world as it is. Living with God is a matter of trust, and the best way to prove the strength of any relationship is to live it and not to put it constantly to the test.

The problem of evil

The existence of evil and suffering in the world is a problem that has vexed Christians for two millennia. In his short meditation penned in the immediate aftermath of 9/11, Rowan Williams tells of how he was stopped in the street in New York on the morning after by a man who 'wanted to know what the hell God was doing when the planes hit the towers' (Williams 2002:7). Similar questions have been asked throughout the long and painful history of humanity by those who hold to a belief in an all-loving and all-powerful God. In the days following 9/11 it was asked – perhaps for the very first time – by those of a new generation for whom the Holocaust is a history lesson and for whom this was the most terrifyingly real evidence of a force of evil in the world and of the enormity of the suffering that such evil can wreak. If God is all-loving then he would not have wanted this to happen, and if he is all-powerful then he would have been able to prevent it from happening. So God is either *not* all-loving or *not* all-powerful, and this is 'the problem of evil'. In a moment we shall look at the main Christian responses to evil and suffering, but there are two points about evil itself that are perhaps worth making beforehand.

Firstly, what is 'evil'? It could simply be said that evil is 'the absence of good'. If I do not fulfil the nature that God has intended for me, or if I choose to be less than God made me to be, then there is the absence of good. If God is good and made humankind in his image and likeness (Genesis 1.26) then evil is whatever hinders the realization of good. Because any vision of God in human form is inappropriate – God is non-material or spiritual – to say that we are made 'in the image of God' must mean in a way that transcends physical appearance. Perhaps we could say that we were made to *be* like God, to know him and to love him as he knows and loves us, and to reflect his love and goodness to the rest of God's creation. God works through people.

Secondly, it will be helpful here to make a distinction between 'moral evil' and 'natural evil'. Although evil is not the same as pain and suffering – the pain experienced by picking up a hot plate is good because it makes us drop it before it burns our fingers – the problem of evil is closely associated with the problem of suffering, because when people become evil this will almost certainly be made manifest in the hurting of others. This is what is called 'moral evil'. Not all suffering, however, is caused by deliberate acts by human beings who have chosen to be less than what God intended them to be. A great deal of the suffering in the world is caused by events for which human beings cannot be held responsible – for example disease, hurricanes, and earthquakes – and these are what we call 'natural evils'.

Christian responses to evil and suffering
Any attempt to defend God in the face of evil in the world is called 'theodicy'. The first of the two classical Christian theodicies was that of Irenaeus (130-202) who believed that God is responsible for the existence of evil in the world, that the world with its good and evil existing together is all part of God's plan and purpose; evil and suffering are necessary conditions for the spiritual growth and development of human beings into the perfect creatures God wants us to be. This present life is a time of trial, perfecting us for future glory in God's kingdom, and the Bible tells us that Jesus himself was made 'perfect through sufferings' (Hebrews 2.10).

Although Irenaeus had nothing to say about animal suffering (perhaps he believed animals have no place in the kingdom of heaven and therefore no need of such improvement) the argument has its followers, not least the many Christians who would say that their relationship with God has been strongest in times of pain and suffering. It is a way in which we learn to acknowledge our need of God; it reminds us of our dependence on him rather than on ourselves and worldly things. On the other hand, Irenaeus' theodicy is unpalatable to many in its attempt to justify evil as being of divine purpose – something good and God-willed. We only have to think of evil and suffering on such a scale as the Holocaust to ask whether an all-loving and all-powerful God could possibly have allowed this to happen for some greater and ennobling purpose. Rabbi Irving Greenberg has given Christians a stark and graphic steer on this: 'No statement, theological or otherwise, should be made that would not be credible in the presence of the burning children' (Rittner et al 2000:41).

The second of the two classical Christian theodicies was that of Augustine of Hippo (354-430), later taken up and developed by Thomas Aquinas (1225-74), and usually called the 'free will defence'. Augustine sought to remove any responsibility for the existence of moral evil from God, placing it instead on Adam and Eve who misused the gift of free will given to them by God. If our love of God and one another is to be authentic it must be freely chosen, and God's love for us respects free will rather than seeks to control. God created the world good, free from the contamination of evil, but he also allowed human beings the freedom to love or not to love – and it is our choosing the latter that gives rise to moral evil.

Aquinas also addressed the problem of natural evil. Although moral evil is not of God's making natural evil can be traced to the instrumentality of God. However, natural evils only *appear* to be evils because we see them from a limited perspective – that is to say from a purely human-centered viewpoint. From God's perspective they are a necessary part of the whole system of creation and are perfectly good. A volcano, for example, which may from time to time cause death and destruction on a massive scale, acts as a giant pressure valve to release an excess of energy built up in the earth's core; it is a vital component of a well-designed planet and does not in any way fall short of what God intended it to be.

As regards animal suffering, this may arise either from

humankind's misuse of free will or as part of God's overall plan for his creation. In the case of the latter, the fact that foxes eat rabbits is part of God's plan to prevent rabbits overrunning the countryside and to sustain the population of foxes; it only appears evil from a rabbit-centered viewpoint, and God is concerned for the whole of his creation.

The Augustine/Aquinas theodicy has much to recommend it, but many feel it is still lacking. It merely transfers any blame from God who then appears to stand back and watch impassively. It seems to portray God as being untouched or untroubled by the pain and suffering caused by evil; it does not speak in any way about God's love, concern and commitment to his creatures; neither does it take account of the God who suffers with his creation. In short, it says nothing about what Christ is meant to have revealed of God's nature. So is there not a better way?

The 'problem of evil' revolves around two basic assumptions – that God is *both* all-loving *and* all-powerful. If we were able to give up one of these assumptions then evil would no longer be a 'problem'. The first assumption – that God is all-loving – is not one that we can ever give up, but the notion of the omnipotence of God is one that we need to think through quite carefully. If God's omnipotence is defended, then God becomes responsible for everything bad that ever happens and for everything good that doesn't happen, and then his goodness is compromised.

The clearest revelation we have of the nature, purposes and activity of God was his revelation to the world in Christ, and so the idea of the omnipotence of God must always be understood in the light of this revelation. Jesus' power was shown in weakness not in strength, in serving others rather than being served by others. His death on the cross was a willing surrender of power, which means that earthly power is in fact no power at all because God's power takes the form of death and God's victory appears only through death. The God who suffered rejection and hatred, loneliness and despair, agonizing pain and death on a cross does not appear to be an omnipotent God at all. God is only revealed as God in the cross of Jesus Christ, a God of abundant, vulnerable and suffering love, who is *present* in the world's pain and joins us in protest against it. 'My God, my God, why have you forsaken me?' (Matthew 27.46). This is a theodicy that has at its heart a weak and suffering God, which seeks not to defend or justify God's action or inaction in the world but to protest against evil and create a motive to overcome it. To be afflicted by evil is not to be afflicted by God but to be appointed in Christ to join God's fight to conquer evil wherever it is to be found. We will return to this in Chapter Four, but now we need to consider one more issue that arises in the group session.

Darwin and Malthus

In 1838, Darwin read a paper by the Reverend Thomas Malthus entitled *Essay on the Principle of Population* (1798), which influenced him greatly. Malthus' argument was simple: human population growth was infinitely greater than the resources of the planet could sustain, yet humankind's urge to increase the species persisted nevertheless because it was driven by a powerful instinct. As a result, the population would be kept in check by other interventions, natural or human, for example plagues, famines, and wars. The 'struggle for existence' that was such an integral part of Darwin's theory of evolution by natural selection was, in his own words, 'the doctrine of Malthus applied with manifold force to the whole animal and vegetable kingdoms' (Darwin 1998:51). The reality of life that Malthus had espoused was the complete opposite of Paley's 'happy world of delighted existence'.

It seemed, then, to Darwin that all the waste and suffering in the natural world were necessary features of life rather than avoidable evils. But was natural selection worth the cost? Was it a legitimate means of creating the higher animals – 'the highest good which we can conceive'? Was it worth all the misery along the way? After much soul searching Darwin ultimately believed it was.

Opponents of religion might say that all this misery is enough to disprove the existence of God. Religious opponents of evolutionary theory, on the other hand, would contend that God would never have created human beings in this random and wasteful way. The trail of pain and destruction over hundreds of millions of years would never have been part of God's plan for the creation of human life. There was, they will argue, a better way – a more 'Godly' way: God created us in the beginning as we are now. *Homo sapiens* is the special creation of a loving God who meant us to be here, rather than the product of indeterminate chance and so much misery along the way.

But neither the randomness nor the suffering actually rules out the presence and activity of God. In fact it could be said that the very opposite of this – an entirely non-random process with no pain and suffering involved – is what would rule out any active involvement by God. God would simply set a perfect process in motion at the start and then sit back and do nothing. This is a belief system known as 'deism': God acted in the past, but no longer acts in the present; God created the universe, but is unable to intervene in the workings of the universe. Deism has no place in Christian theology (cf. theism), because Christianity regards the continuing presence and activity of God in the world to be an essential element of belief.

The history of the world is as it is because of a series of chance events. History is not planned in advance; rather it is the trail of consequences arising from unforeseeable happenings. Had Archduke Franz Ferdinand of Austria not been assassinated in Sarajevo in June 1914 then the First World War might never have happened and the whole history of the twentieth century would have turned out differently: no humiliating defeat of Germany; no rise of Nazism; no Second World War; no Holocaust; no spread of Communism and so forth. The world we live in today would be very different from how it actually is, for better or for worse. But God is still involved in history. The personal experiences of life cannot be isolated from the breadth of the total experience of human history; rather they are set in the broad context of history in which we participate as people of our own time. God participates in individual human experiences, and so God shares in history and reveals himself to us as one who has been involved in history.

If that is so for the history of the world, then why should it not be so for the *natural* history of the world? If history is unpredictable, contingent upon a series of chance events in which we recognize that God is nevertheless present and active, then why should it be any different for the biological history of the creation of humankind?

Group Session

0.00 Bible Study
Where is the devil quoting from and where is Jesus quoting from? Find the texts and look them up. What happened at Massah? Can you think of any occasions when you have put God to the test? **10 minutes**

0.10 Film Clip 1
The Darwin family goes on a picnic with friends Joseph Hooker and the Reverend John Innes. **5 minutes**

0.15 Brainstorm
What did you find interesting or thought-provoking in that clip? What issues or questions does it raise for you? What would you like to come back to later if there is time? **5 minutes**

0.20 Group Discussion
Darwin asks Innes for his response to all the waste and

destruction in nature, and Innes replies, 'that's the beauty of God's plan'. Which theodicy is Innes holding to here? Darwin replies, 'it's an exceedingly wasteful plan – these myriad lives created only to be immediately extinguished'. How would you respond to Darwin? Do you think God could have created human life (or something like it) in a quicker, less costly, or less random way? **10 minutes**

0.30 In Small Groups
What do you think God was doing when the planes hit the twin towers of the World Trade Center on 11 September 2001? What problems are associated with any suggestion that God should interfere in human actions? How does God act in the world if not by direct intervention? **10 minutes**

0.40 Feedback and Share
Leader: allow each small group to feedback and share with everyone else some of the things they have talked about. **5 minutes**

0.45 Film Clip 2
Darwin and Annie undergo hydrotherapy at Dr. James Gully's Malvern clinic in March 1851. **5 minutes**

0.50 Brainstorm
What did you find interesting or thought-provoking in that clip? What issues or questions does it raise for you? What would you like to come back to later if there is time? **5 minutes**

0.55 Group Discussion
Darwin prays, 'If it is in your power, God, to save her, then I will believe in you for the rest of my days'. Is it in God's power to save Annie? How do you think God might react to being put to the test like this? He adds, 'Take me, if you must take someone,

but not her'. What does this say about his view of God at this point in his life? **10 minutes**

1.05 In Small Groups
How should we pray? Why does it sometimes appear that God hasn't heard us? How does God answer our prayers? **10 minutes**

1.15 Feedback and Share
Leader: allow each small group to feedback and share with everyone else some of the things they have talked about. **5 minutes**

1.20 Meditation and Prayer

Reader 1

Who has believed what we have heard? And to whom has the arm of the LORD been revealed? For he grew up before him like a young plant, and like a root out of dry ground; he had no form or majesty that we should look at him, nothing in his appearance that we should desire him. He was despised and rejected by others; a man of suffering and acquainted with infirmity; and as one from whom others hide their faces he was despised, and we held him of no account.

Surely he has born our infirmities and carried our diseases; yet we accounted him stricken, struck down by God, and afflicted. But he was wounded for our transgressions, crushed for our iniquities; upon him was the punishment that made us whole, and by his bruises we are healed. (Isaiah 53.1-5)

Pause

When Jesus entered Peter's house, he saw his mother-in-law lying in bed with a fever; he touched her hand, and the fever left her, and she got up and began to serve him. That evening they brought to him many who were possessed with demons; and he cast out the spirits with a word, and cured all who were sick. This was to fulfill what had been spoken through the prophet Isaiah, "He took our infirmities and bore our diseases." (Matthew 8.14-17)

Pause

Before God and with God we live without God. God lets himself be pushed out of the world on to the cross. He is weak and powerless in the world, and that is precisely the way, the only way, in which he is with us and helps us. Matt[hew] 8.17 makes it quite clear that Christ helps us, not by virtue of his omnipotence, but by virtue of his weakness and suffering. (Dietrich Bonhoeffer, 1944, in Bonhoeffer 2001:134)

One minute's silence for reflection

Reader 2

An extract from *Love's Endeavour, Love's Expense* by the Reverend W. H. Vanstone:

I dreamed: and in my dream a rubbish-collector came to me and told me that he had been clearing up after a riot; and I myself saw the huge pile of stones and cans and waste paper and scrap metal which he had collected. Then the man touched my arm and said, 'But what am I to do? For deep within the pile, buried at the bottom of it, I have seen a living face'. Though my own eyes did not see the face, I knew in my dream that it must be the face of God.

A few hours later, when I preached in Church, I was compelled to speak of my dream. For it seemed to suggest a different way in which the truth of Christmas might have been disclosed – a harrowing and appalling way. It made one newly sensitive to, and grateful for, the graciousness of the way in which the truth of Christmas is in fact disclosed to us. But, in substance, it was the same truth. It was the truth of a God Who, in love, is totally expended for the being of His creation – so that He is helpless under its weight and barely survives for its everlasting support; so that, in the tragedies of the creation, in its waste and rubbish, God Himself is exposed to tragedy: so that the creation is sustained at the cost of the agony of One Who is buried and almost wholly submerged within the depth of it. (Vanstone 1977:71-72)

One minute's silence for reflection

Reader 3

An extract from *The Hardest Part* by the Reverend G. A. Studdert Kennedy:

The difficulty really [is] in the attempt to see in Nature an Almighty God – a Being Who can do everything which we imagine to be possible, a God Who could have made a perfect, painless, sinless world at a stroke, but Who, for some inexplicable reason, chose to adopt this slow, tortuous, and painful method of evolutionary creation. We are invited to find a meaning and a use for everything in Nature – even sharks and poisonous snakes. We are asked to regard floods, famines, pestilence, and disease as visitations of the Almighty, exhibitions of His supreme power. We are told that Nature is a perfect system of balances in which there is a place for everything and everything has its place. There is supposed to be no failure and no possibility of failure in Nature, inasmuch as every detail of it is the work of absolute omnipotence. The result of this attempt to adapt Nature to an imaginary conception of God based upon abstractions is utter bewilderment. The materialism of Haeckel and the pseudo-Darwinites seems honest and illuminating beside it. (Studdert Kennedy 2007:20)

One minute's silence for reflection

Reader 4

O Jesus,
insulted, mocked, and spit upon,
have mercy upon me
and let me run with patience the race set before me.
O Jesus,
dragged to the pillar, scourged, and bathed in blood,
have mercy upon me
and let me not faint in the fiery trial...
O Jesus,
hanging on the accursed tree, bowing the head, giving up the
    ghost,
have mercy upon me
and conform my whole soul to thy holy, humble, suffering
    Spirit.
(John Wesley, 1733)

Week Five: The Devil Returns

Then Satan entered into Judas called Iscariot, who was one of the twelve; he went away and conferred with the chief priests and officers of the temple police about how he might betray [Jesus] to them. They were greatly pleased and agreed to give him money. So he consented and began to look for an opportunity to betray him to them when no crowd was present. (Luke 22.3-6)

Prelude

In the third and final temptation, which we read last week, Jesus was tempted to call upon God to deliver him from death in Jerusalem. There is irony in that for, as we know, Jesus eventually does face death in Jerusalem when the devil returns, and he chooses not his own deliverance but faithfulness to his Father's will. He will fulfill his divine Sonship not by escaping death, but by accepting it. Whereas we in our baptism die to our earthly life and are born into the new life of Christ, the process for Jesus is apparently reversed: he renounces his divine life of heavenly perfection and power, and accepts the burden of human life and weakness. God the creator of all things chooses to live in us, the creatures that he has made.

As Holy Week draws closer we need to think about the question: why did Jesus die on the cross? 'That's easy,' you might say, 'he died to save us from our sins.' That is undoubtedly right, and that is what the Bible says (e.g. Matthew 1.21), but what does it actually mean? One of the reasons why evolution troubled the Victorian Church was that it raised some questions about this basic tenet of Christian belief. Augustine of Hippo, as we saw last week, located the origin of moral evil in the Fall when Satan lured Adam and Eve away from obedience to God. God had created the world good and free from the contamination of evil, but satanic temptation led to humanity's disobedience and sinfulness. The consequence of sin was death (Genesis 2.17 and 3.19), and the cross of Jesus served to effect a reversal of the Fall. In St Paul's words, 'for the wages of sin is death, but the free gift of God is eternal life in Christ Jesus our Lord' (Romans 6.23). And this is Paul again: 'for as all die in Adam, so all will be made alive in Christ' (1 Corinthians 15.22). But if humanity never did actually hold a position of primal innocence in the first place – having evolved from anthropoid apes only in the very recent history of the world – then there was no Fall, and if there was no Fall how can it be said that Christ came to 'undo' the effects of original sin?

Furthermore, if the knowledge of good and evil cannot be located in the Fall it must have developed as a natural instinct in humans. If humans are simply animals among other animals, sharing a common nature and mental qualities and having a mind that has developed from the mind of the lower animals, is it not possible that other sentient beings could have developed the same instinct and also be capable of choosing evil over good? Are not animals, therefore, also in need of being saved from death – the consequence of sin? Why should the human race hold such a unique place in God's plan for salvation?

The Fall and original sin

Augustine was probably the greatest and most influential mind of the Western/Roman Church. He regarded the 'original sin' of Adam and Eve to be an inherited guilt, as if it were somehow transmitted through the generations. 'The human nature by which each one of us is now born of Adam requires a physician because it is not healthy,' he wrote, and 'our guilty nature is liable to a just penalty.' We were all *born* sinners.

The Eastern/Greek Church, however, takes on a more guarded interpretation of original sin. In the Orthodox tradition it is not regarded in quasi-biological terms as an inherited guilt, as Bishop Kallistos Ware explains:

This picture, which normally passes for the Augustinian view, is unacceptable to Orthodoxy. The doctrine of original sin means rather that we are born into an environment where it is easy to do evil and hard to do good; easy to hurt others, and hard to heal their wounds; easy to arouse men's suspicions, and hard to win their trust. (Ware 1995:62)

This is a helpful definition because it means that in the light of evolutionary science, we do not have to rely for an answer to the question 'why did Jesus die?' on imaginary characters that are part of a creation myth. Nevertheless, we cannot ignore the truth that we are born into a world of accumulated wrong-doing to which we add by our own accumulation of wrongs. Sin is what separates us from God, but the Christian conception of 'sin' is not particularly one of individual sinful acts. When John the Baptist proclaims Jesus as 'the Lamb of God who takes away the sin of the world' (John 1.29) his use of the singular word 'sin' emphasizes the world's collective brokenness rather than individual human sins. Sin is a relational problem; sin means ignoring God in the world that God has made, which is exactly what Adam and Eve did and which is why their story is still of value to us at a figurative level rather than a literal one. Sin also implies a state of hostility between humanity and God, between human being and human being, and between humanity and the rest of God's creation. The cross of Jesus is an expression of God's grace bringing peace and healing to all these wounded relationships. The cross was God's embrace.

This is the language of 'reconciliation' much favoured by Paul: 'God was in Christ reconciling the world to himself' (2 Corinthians 5.19), not counting our trespasses against us. God wants to embrace us in the outpouring of his love for us, for us to embrace one another made in the image of God, and for us to embrace the whole of God's creation. The cross offers us outstretched arms, and the death of Jesus is the ultimate expression of a life lived on behalf of others. We are reconciled to God now, through the cross, for our future redemption when Christ comes again.

Human salvation

In the Biblical language of 'redemption' we find images of being released or set free. Salvation means deliverance or liberation from evil, sin, and death, and for this we must wait until Christ comes again. The idea that when we die our souls are released to live with God for eternity is a false belief, which was absorbed from Greek philosophy (Plato) and found its way into Christian thought when the early Church spread into the Greco-Roman world. The New Testament vision is of a bodily resurrection: when the trumpet sounds the dead will be raised, clothed in new and imperishable bodies appropriate for life in a new created order (1 Corinthians 15.52). In this new creation, the marriage of heaven and earth, death and mourning and crying and pain will be no more (Revelation 21.4). Tom Wright defines heaven as 'God's dimension of present reality' (Wright 2006:7). It is not a place, and when we die we do not 'go to heaven' as if we are literally whisked away to some distant place in the sky. Death-sleep-resurrection is the pattern revealed in the New Testament, where 'sleep' might be taken to mean 'rest in the peace of Christ' until the day of resurrection. Jesus described this state as being 'in Paradise' (Luke 23.43). When Christ comes again the kingdom of heaven (or the kingdom of God) comes to us. If heaven is not a place then the kingdom, too, is not a place; it is better understood to mean the kingly reign or rule of God. In the Lord's Prayer this is what we pray will come 'on earth as it is in heaven', and this is what will come upon us in the great renewal of all things, a totally renewed creation marked by the personal presence of Jesus himself, a kingdom which Jesus first reveals and rules before handing his reign over to the Father (1 Corinthians 15.24). The new creation is not the *replacement* of the present creation but its *renewal*, the eternal future of the present world in which we live.

In the Biblical notion of salvation, human beings are saved by God's grace alone, to the exclusion of all human merit. The pre-Reformation Roman Catholic Church came to the point of subverting the doctrine of grace through its obsession with 'works' – acts of penance for individual sins, acts of merit and acts of benevolence – all for the purpose of earning a place in heaven. The idea of forgiveness by grace had been corrupted by the purchase of God's favour. Through his reading of Romans 1.16-17 Martin Luther asserted that salvation is God's free and gracious gift given to humankind in the atoning work of Christ; it is not something that can be bought or earned. It can only be accepted – through faith alone – or rejected.

Faith is not just a warm emotional feeling. It is not 'blind hope', neither is it simply the belief that there is a God. Faith is a trust in the promises of God, a trust demonstrated in obedient action and an open-minded acceptance of God's hidden work. It is a steadfast confidence in God's purposes, and a life lived in the light of that confidence. Faith is believing that there is more to life than meets the eye, a way of living that treats what is seen now as revealing what is to come. It is placing trust in something that is greater and more permanent, towards which we can move.

As a result of the Reformers' focus on the dynamic relationship between faith and grace, Protestantism came to place its emphasis almost solely upon personal salvation. Inadvertently its theology and liturgy became a nuanced version of the prior Roman Catholic preoccupation with individual human sins and individual human salvation. Although new vigour was given to the doctrine of grace, a high price was paid for this victory. An understanding of the cosmic or universal significance of Christ's saving work – retained in both the Orthodox and Celtic traditions to this day – was all but lost.

The cosmic scope of salvation

An acceptance of evolution does nothing to detract from anything that has been said above about human salvation. What it does do, however, is encourage us to ask whether human beings *alone* have a place in God's plan for salvation, and to ask whether Christ came into the world *only* for the purpose of 'saving us from our sins'. Did the incarnation happen solely to free fallen humanity from the bondage of sin? Would God the Son have become incarnate in Jesus of Nazareth if humankind had never sinned? The Bible tells us he would. It tells us that the incarnation was more than just a response to a particular human need; rather it was the ultimate self-revelation of a loving God to the world. Through Jesus' life and death we gain a glimpse of the character of God: the Son reveals the Father. The Fourth Gospel in particular makes ample use of the language of revelation – ignorance and knowing, blindness and seeing. The incarnation raises humanity to a higher level, a more Christ-like state than before, because in Jesus we see the full possibilities of our human nature.

The Bible also tells us that God intended the incarnation and self-sacrifice of the Son from eternity to perfect and complete creation. Revelation 13.8 speaks of 'the Lamb that was slaughtered from the foundation of the world', and Matthew 25.34 of 'the kingdom prepared for you from the foundation of the world'. The incarnation was more than simply God's response to the predicament of humanity; rather it was in some way part of the eternal purpose of God. It would have happened even if the human race had remained free from sin. It was an essential stage in humanity's journey towards the realization of its potential to God-given life, in moving from the divine image to the divine likeness. And this journey towards perfection and completion is not the journey of humanity alone but of all created matter, which must have its destiny too.

If God loves, values and cherishes everything he has made it can scarcely be possible that everything of it except human life is consigned to decay and death. God has a plan for the whole created order that is as comprehensive as his plan for the human race. When Paul spoke of 'redemption' he had in mind a vaster and more glorious concept than the salvation of human beings alone:

> I consider that the sufferings of this present time are not worth comparing with the glory about to be revealed to us. For the creation waits with eager longing for the revealing of the children of God; for the creation was subjected to futility, not of its own will but by the will of the one who subjected it, in hope that the creation itself will be set free from its bondage to decay and will obtain the freedom of the glory of the children of God. We know that the whole creation has been groaning in labour pains until now; and not only the creation, but we ourselves, who have the first fruits of the Spirit, groan inwardly while we wait for adoption, the redemption of our bodies. (Romans 8.18-23)

The experience of the Holy Spirit is a ground of hope for the whole universe. Humankind cannot be isolated from the rest of creation, and Paul gives us a sense of God's deliverance on a cosmic scale. The universe, too, is waiting for something. In the time to come it will be transfigured, but for this we must wait – like a woman awaiting the birth of a child.

The victory of the cross is understood to extend to the entire created order. There is inter-relatedness and interdependence between all created things – something that evolutionary science spells out so clearly – and a unity at the very heart of the cosmos. The cross stands between creation-in-the-beginning and the cosmic goal that awaits it – 'a new heaven and a new earth' (Revelation 21.1). And so nothing of this world will be lost; everything of value in God's good and present creation, all that God himself treasures, will not disappear into nothingness but will be transformed into something new and better and gathered into God's eternal future. That is God's promise, 'to make all things new' (Revelation 21.5), and the creatures that helped us get where we are today can surely not be excluded from that.

Group Session

0.00 Bible Study
Judas was 'one of the twelve' – can you name the other eleven disciples/apostles? Who replaced Judas as one of the twelve before Pentecost? Do you find it helpful or unhelpful to think of evil personified in a character called 'the devil' or 'Satan'? **10 minutes**

0.10 Film Clip 1
Annie dies. **5 minutes**
Leader: after viewing this clip, don't rush into the brainstorming. Allow time for the group to absorb slowly what they have seen. It may be appropriate to keep a time of silent or open prayer.

0.15 Brainstorm
What did you find interesting or thought-provoking in that clip? What issues or questions does it raise for you? What would you like to come back to later if there is time? **5 minutes**

0.20 Group Discussion
Why do you think Annie wanted to hear the story about Jenny's death? Darwin tells Annie that Jenny looked into her keeper's eyes 'in a most human fashion, and then she laid her head against him and died'. How does this inform your under-standing of evolution? Do you feel any differently now from how you did in Week One about sharing a common ancestry with the anthropoid apes? **10 minutes**

0.30 In Small Groups

What has struck you most about everything you have learned in this course about evolutionary science and the Church? Do you feel more confident now about finding some common ground between God and evolution? If you were to have a discussion with a creationist tomorrow, what are the main points you would wish to try to get across? **10 minutes**

0.40 Feedback and Share

Leader: allow each small group to feedback and share with everyone else some of the things they have talked about. **5 minutes**

0.45 Film Clip 2

Dr. Gully tries to comfort Darwin after Annie's death. **5 minutes**

0.50 Brainstorm

What did you find interesting or thought-provoking in that clip? What issues or questions does it raise for you? What would you like to come back to later if there is time? **5 minutes**

0.55 Group Discussion

Gully says that Annie is 'in heaven' – what does he mean? Do you think that Jenny is in heaven too? Gully also says: 'You say you take no comfort from religion, but do you have faith?' What point is Gully trying to make here? **10 minutes**

1.05 In Small Groups

Do you feel more confident now about talking to others about 'the problem of pain'? Try to do it now: where is God in all the pain of his creation? How can all the suffering in the world be reconciled with an all-loving and all-powerful God who made the world? **10 minutes**

1.15 Feedback and Share

Leader: allow each small group to feedback and share with everyone else some of the things they have talked about. **5 minutes**

1.20 Meditation and Prayer

Reader 1

Let the same mind be in you that was in Christ Jesus, who, though he was in the form of God, did not regard equality with God as something to be exploited, but emptied himself, taking the form of a slave, being born in human likeness. And being found in human form, he humbled himself and became obedient to the point of death – even death on a cross. (Philippians 2.5-8)

Pause

It is indeed right and good to give you thanks and praise, almighty God and everlasting Father, through Jesus Christ your Son. For when he humbled himself to come among us in human flesh, he fulfilled the plan you formed before the foundation of the world to open for us the way of salvation. Confident that your promise will be fulfilled, we now watch for the day when Christ our Lord will come again in glory. (Extended Preface for Advent, *Common Worship: Services and Prayers for the Church of England*)

Pause

Blessed be the God and Father of our Lord Jesus Christ! By his great mercy he has given us a new birth into a living hope through the resurrection of Jesus Christ from the dead, and into an inheritance that is imperishable, undefiled, and unfading, kept in heaven for you, who are being protected by the power of God through faith for a salvation ready to be revealed in the last time. (1 Peter 1.3-5)

One minute's silence for reflection

Reader 2

An extract from *The Trinity and the Kingdom of God* by Jürgen Moltmann, Emeritus Professor of Systematic Theology at the University of Tübingen, Germany:

> Even if we make the 'emergency' of human sin the starting point, so as to grasp the necessity of divine reconciliation, and in order to expect the coming of the divine Reconciler, we must go beyond the measure of human need if we are to understand grace as *God's* grace...
>
> According to Paul Christ was not merely 'delivered for our offences' but was also 'raised again for our justification' (Rom. 4.25 AV). Reconciling sinners with God through his cross, he brings about the new righteousness, the new life, the new creature through his resurrection. The justification of the sinner is more than merely the forgiveness of sins. It leads to new life: 'Where sin increased, grace abounded all the more' (Rom. 5.20). This is the way Paul expresses the imbalance between sin and grace, and the *added value* of grace. This surplus of grace over and above the forgiveness of sins and the reconciliation of sinners, represents the power of the new creation which consummates creation-in-the-beginning. It follows from this that the Son of God did not become man simply because of the sin of men and women, but rather for the sake of perfecting creation. (Moltmann 1981:115-116)

One minute's silence for reflection

Reader 3

An extract from *Hope against Hope* by Richard Bauckham, Professor of New Testament Studies at the University of St Andrews, and Trevor Hart, Professor of Divinity at the University of St Andrews:

> [The] Christian hope that the whole created reality will be renewed by God, glorified by his presence and taken into union with his own eternal life has maintained only a rather tenuous hold on the Christian imagination for much of Christian history. It is perhaps here that the legacy of Platonism in the Christian tradition has had its most extensive effect. The bulwark which the dogmatic affirmation of bodily resurrection has with difficulty maintained against the complete spiritualizing of human destiny has been less effective against the persistent tendency to understand human destiny as a destiny apart from the rest of creation. Human nature has been so abstracted from its continuity and solidarity with the rest of the material creation that its distinctiveness – in rationality and awareness of God – has been misunderstood as its unique fitness for eternity. So the Christian hope has constantly been understood as hope for human fulfilment in another world ('heaven') rather than as hope for the eternal future of this world in which we live...
>
> If God's creation is ultimately only a throw-away world, destined to perish when its purpose as a vale of human soul-making is fulfilled, it may not seem to matter too much what we do with it. (Bauckham and Hart 1999:128-129)

One minute's silence for reflection

Reader 4

Loving God, we give you thanks and praise
for all that you have done for us.
For your whole created universe bursting with life and infinite
possibilities,
a universe created and yet still being created.
For the beauty and fragility of our spinning planet,
the blue oceans, swarming with life, and the green and
verdant earth.
For our fellow human beings, people of many colours, of
many languages,
of many abilities, yet all your children.
We give you thanks for the life, death, and resurrection
of your Son, Jesus Christ.
For the message which he brings, for the life in us which he
renews,
and the example he has given us to follow.
We give you thanks for the Holy Spirit,
sweeping through all of life with boundless energy,
at once as gentle as the breath of a child, and yet as fierce as a
raging storm,
lifting us up in your grace.
(Prayer of Thanksgiving in *Worship: from the United Reformed
Church*)

Chapter Four

A Theology of a Suffering God

The year after Charles Darwin died, a man was born who was to have a seminal role in the development of a 'new orthodoxy' in Christian thought. At the end of Weeks Three and Four of the course you read an extract from *The Hardest Part*, a collection of essays published in 1918 by the Reverend G. A. Studdert Kennedy, MC (1883-1929). Studdert Kennedy is widely known as the priest and poet 'Woodbine Willie', the affectionate name given to him by the men with whom he served in France during the Great War 1914-18. He is remembered also as a gifted preacher and orator of exceptional eloquence and power who had a rare ability to communicate his understanding of God to ordinary people and to make God 'real' to the many to whom he seemed to be dead. He happens to be a great hero of mine, someone who perhaps more than any other has informed my knowledge, understanding, and love of God, and I believe that his prose and poetry deserve to be more widely read.

He was a theologian of creativity and originality whose writings were dominated by the severe theological and ethical struggles with the experience of war. It was theology quite literally forged in fields of fire. For him, the great illumination came from the realization that God does not watch our suffering from afar, untouched and untroubled by it, but himself suffers in, with and for his creation. The cross became the centre of all his faith in God, and a theodicy with a weak and suffering God at its heart was central to his thought. His thoughts and ideas received a mixed reception in his own lifetime but were later taken up by others who themselves sought to address the involvement of God in the sufferings of humanity as the horrors of war and the Holocaust darkened the world once again.

The Reverend G. A. Studdert Kennedy

Studdert Kennedy's life can be divided into three distinctive parts: 1) the pre-war years 1883-1913, during which he answered the call to ordination and began his ministry; 2) the war years 1914-18, during which he served as a military chaplain in France; and 3) the post-war years 1919-29, during which he worked principally as chief missioner for the Industrial Christian Fellowship.

The Pre-War Years 1883-1913

Geoffrey Anketell Studdert Kennedy was born in his father's vicarage in Leeds on 27 June 1883, the seventh of nine children born to Joan and the Reverend William Studdert Kennedy. William was an Irishman, fifty-eight years old when Geoffrey was born and in his second marriage, and his parish Quarry Hill in Leeds was said to be one of the worst slums in the north of England.

Geoffrey was educated at a private preparatory school before being sent to Leeds Grammar School and Trinity College, Dublin. At Leeds Grammar he became friends with another boy by the name of J. K. Mozley, who would go on to become Chancellor of St. Paul's Cathedral and publish a book *The Impassibility of God* (1926). The question of whether God is personally involved in the sufferings of creation, or whether he is beyond the reach of all emotion and pain, was a question the two often debated together, and a search for an answer to the question remained a preoccupation for Studdert Kennedy.

He was awarded a First in Classics and Divinity at Trinity College in 1904, and in the following year joined the teaching staff at Calday Grange Grammar School in Cheshire where he spent two and a half years teaching general subjects. In 1907 he abandoned teaching and entered the Ripon Clergy College for a nine-month course. He was ordained deacon in Worcester Cathedral in 1908 at the age of twenty-four.

Studdert Kennedy was appointed to his first post as curate at Rugby Parish Church, where he quickly earned a reputation for being wild, mentally undisciplined, in many ways foolish, yet at the same time extraordinarily eloquent. He was of generally comical appearance, 'a sad clown on God's stage' (Grundy 1997:9). He seemed to gravitate naturally to the slum area of Sun Court where he had a bed-sit, and would wander in and out of the pubs talking to the men. A deep love of the poor would distinguish his life to the end.

He remained in Rugby for four years during which, after two years in the diaconate, he was ordained priest. In 1912 he returned to Quarry Hill to assist his aged father as curate in place of his younger brother Cecil, who resigned Holy Orders to join the Church of Christ Scientist, one of several in the family who joined the sect of 'Christian Science' founded in the USA in 1866. There he fell in love and married Emily Catlow and remained there until the death of his father in 1914.

The War Years 1914-18

With the death of his father, the whole point of returning to Leeds was gone and in June 1914, just two months before Britain's declaration of war on Germany, he was instituted to the living of St. Paul's, Worcester, a poor parish with a small income. He chose the place largely for that reason, and the poverty he actually encountered there sowed the seeds of his radical political opinions of later years as a champion of Christian Socialism.

On the outbreak of war, whilst urging that every able-bodied man should volunteer for service (something he came to regret when the war was over), he tried to get into the army himself. That meant a chaplaincy to the forces, something by no means easy to attain: he had to make provision for his duties in Worcester to be carried out in his absence, persuade his bishop to release him, and commend himself to the military authorities. All this he managed to accomplish, and on 21 December 1915 he was appointed Temporary Chaplain to the Forces. On Christmas Day he was in France.

> Thus began the wartime ministry of a man destined to become, through personal qualities and the accident of circumstances, the most celebrated army padre of all time: and one who was to end hating with a rare bitterness the whole enterprise to which, at this beginning, he went with such naïvety. (Purcell 1983:98)

Stationed initially in a railway siding in Rouen, it was his custom to spend many hours in the canteen with the men awaiting transport to the front, and then go with them to the train distributing Bibles from one haversack and Woodbine cigarettes from another, which is how he came to earn the nickname 'Woodbine Willie'.

In June 1916, in time for the Somme offensive, he was posted to the Western Front as padre with the 157th Brigade of the 46th Division. It was the first of three periods of battle experience, to be followed by the attack on the Messines Ridge in 1917 (where he was awarded the Military Cross for conspicuous gallantry attending the wounded under heavy fire), and the final advance in the last year of the war. Afflicted by severe asthma all his life, he was weakened further by trench fever and gas poisoning.

Between these periods in the front line he was given a series of special postings to three Army Infantry Schools, a School for Physical and Bayonet Training, and the National Mission of Repentance and Hope, where he began writing dialect verse for the inarticulate as a means of getting across something of its message. It was during these postings that he had time to put down on paper his thoughts from the front, which resulted in *The Hardest Part* (1918) and *Rough Rhymes of a Padre* (1918), the profits from which he donated to St. Dunstan's charity for the blind.

The Post-War Years 1919-29

Studdert Kennedy returned from France in March 1919. The post-war years were a difficult time for religion: bereavement, disability, poverty and suffering were everywhere and on an extraordinarily large scale; always there were the unemployed. Although he was still vicar of St. Paul's, Worcester, he had become a national figure: King George V made him a Royal Chaplain, his fame followed him around, and there were many demands on him to speak. In 1922, he resigned the living of St. Paul's, having already become deeply involved in the work of the Industrial Christian Fellowship ('ICF'). He was appointed to the living of St. Edmund King and Martyr, Lombard Street, in the City of London, a parish of very few residents where, as a conse-quence, the pastoral demands were not great. This allowed him to devote himself wholeheartedly to other things, and he took up the position of chief missioner for the ICF.

The ICF was formed just after the First World War out of the merger of the Christian Social Union and the Navvy ['navigation man'] Mission Society, two of many societies that had grown up in the nineteenth century to bring a Christian social conscience to the relentless march of industrialism. The parochial organization of the Church meant it was failing to have any significant impact on daily life in the mills and factories, and it was seen to be out of touch with a very large part of society.

Studdert Kennedy, with his high profile and exceptional ability to get the Christian message across to ordinary men and women, was undoubtedly the right man for the job. But an unceasing workload of rallies and speaking engagements around the country, whilst all the time he was writing, took its toll on his already fragile health. He died in Liverpool of flu-induced pneumonia on 8 March 1929 at the age of 45. He was survived by his wife Emily and three sons, Patrick, Christopher and Michael. William Temple, at the time Archbishop of York and destined to become Archbishop of Canterbury from 1942-4, gave him this epitaph:

> If to be a Priest is to carry others on the heart and offer them with self in the sacrifice of human nature – the Body and the Blood – to God the Father of our Lord Jesus Christ, then Geoffrey Studdert Kennedy was the finest priest that I have known. (Temple 1929:208)

The Theology of G. A. Studdert Kennedy

The Hardest Part, published in 1918, is a collection of nine essays each addressing a particular aspect of how God is known. The book takes its title from one of Studdert Kennedy's own dialect poems, *The Sorrow of God*:

> The sorrows o' God must be 'ard to bear
>   If 'E really 'as Love in 'Is 'eart,
> And the 'ardest part i' the world to play
>   Must surely be God's part.
> (Studdert Kennedy 1927:132)

The essays express the thoughts that came to him amid the hardship of the trenches and the brutal realities of war, which brought him face to face with the problem of reconciling the presence of evil and suffering in the world with the Christian affirmation of the goodness and omnipotence of God who created the world.

At the end of Week Four of this course, you read an extract from the essay entitled 'God in Nature'. Here is some more from that same essay:

Behind all the vast history of effort, ceaseless effort, that Science has disclosed, I can see a will, but not an absolutely omnipotent will that knows no failure and no strain. I cannot see the calm, serene, untroubled potentate whose word at once creates perfection. The paths of natural development are strewn with species that have failed, like the dead horses on the road from Hell-fire Corner to the line...

That is the picture of God which Nature gives you when you look square in her face and refuse to blind yourself either to her failure or her success. God was forced to limit Himself when He undertook the task of material creation. He had to bind Himself with chains and pierce Himself with nails, and take upon Himself the travail pangs of creation. The universe was made as it is because it is the only way it could be made, and this way lays upon God the burden of many failures and of eternal strain – the sorrow of God the Father which Christ revealed. (Studdert Kennedy 2007:22-23)

At the dawn of a new day after a battle, under a red sky on a perfect morning, Studdert Kennedy is moved to ponder the 'unutterable beauty' of nature. He argues that one cannot leave nature out of religion because nature drives human beings to belief in something or someone behind it. The beauty of nature's colours and the music of its sounds call us to worship their Maker in gratitude, to put into words some expression of our love and praise. But nature's many voices seem to contradict one another – there is tenderness and cruelty, order and chaos, beauty and ugliness. If one believes in an Almighty God who could have made a perfect, painless, sinless world at a stroke, then one would curse him for nature's manifest imperfections and many cruelties. There is clearly much here that connects with the observations of Darwin and Malthus on the struggle for existence that rages through all living nature, which we explored in Week Four of the course.

He goes on to argue that the entire created order is the fruit not only of God's power but also of God's pain, the pain of a striving and suffering Creator. But nature's 'horror chambers' are not eternal; just as the cross is followed by an empty tomb and victory, they are only temporary and contingent and God will overcome them in the end. God is striving, suffering, crucified but unconquerable. The truth of God in nature is the truth of Christ crucified and risen again to reveal the suffering but triumphant Father. There is much here that connects with what we explored in Week Five of the course about the cosmic scope of salvation and the renewal of all creation.

Studdert Kennedy's thoughts and ideas about a suffering God and 'God not Almighty' were not well received by some in the English Church establishment in 1918. In response, he was moved to add a postscript to *The Hardest Part*, 'a reply to some criticism and a few words to any readers who may be hurt by what I have written'. His critics cited a partial theology, a distorted truth, a lack of balance, the predominance of the one idea, to which he responded that battles do not make for carefully balanced thought. His style, he said, might be crude and brutal, but it was not as crude as war or as brutal as battle.

There is indeed 'the predominance of the one idea', the same motif continually occurring. It is a theme with which the world of theology today, almost a century on, is greatly familiar, but it is still not without its critics. It is what is called a 'kenotic' Christology – stay with me for this! – by which it is meant that in Christ's *kenosis* or 'self-emptying' (Philippians 2.7) God laid aside the divine attribute of omnipotence. Kenoticism holds that God must limit himself both in creating and sustaining the world and in becoming man. The incarnation itself is dependent upon some type of limitation of God as God: some sort of change is demanded; God must cease to be fully God.

Particular criticism of this will be heard from those who follow the teachings of Thomas Aquinas on the immutability of

God. 'Thomists' (for that is what they are called) vehemently defend the divine attributes of omnipotence, omniscience and omnipresence. These attributes signify what it means for God to be God – to give them up is to cease to be God. Such a change is not only impossible since God is immutable, but it is impossible even to conceive how an omnipotent being can give up or restrain his omnipotence. With an obvious need to address the issue that Jesus Christ was God incarnate and that he suffered and died on the cross, Thomists believe that Christ suffered only in his human nature and not his divine nature. God cannot suffer.

Studdert Kennedy maintained that the thoughts he had written down were not peculiarly his own, that others were beginning to see a fresh vision of God in Christ. 'I believe it is in the minds of thousands', he wrote, 'who have neither time nor words to express it.' And he was right, as developments were taking place elsewhere that would lead to a 'new orthodoxy' in Christian thought. But first, it is necessary to outline Martin Luther's rebuttal of the classic view of the impassibility of God.

Martin Luther's Theologia Crucis

The accepted doctrine of the nature of God was that God was perfect. To be perfect meant being unchanging and self-sufficient, and so it was thought impossible for such a perfect being to be affected or changed by anything outside itself. Philo, the Jewish-Hellenistic philosopher who lived at the time of Christ, wrote a treatise 'That God is unchangeable', vigorously defending the impassibility of God. It may well have been a Hellenistic distortion of an earlier biblical understanding of God as Judaism came into contact with Greek culture and thought, but it seems to have stuck with many earlier Christian writers. Origen alone amongst the theologians of the patristic period countered this view, returning to Old Testament passages which seemed to speak of God's passibility (e.g. Psalm 103.8, Isaiah 49.13). But the view that God lies beyond all human emotion and pain persisted into the Middle Ages with Anselm of Canterbury and Thomas Aquinas both developing this dogma. Anselm, for example, wrote: 'For when you [God] see us in our misery, we experience the effect of compassion; you, however, do not experience this feeling.'

Martin Luther (1483-1546) made his most celebrated protest against the classic view of the impassibility of God in the Heidelberg Disputation of 1518. He contrasted two rival ways of thinking about God, a *theologia gloriae* ('theology of glory') that perceives God's glory, power and wisdom, and a *theologia crucis* ('theology of the cross') that discerns God hidden from us in the suffering of the cross of Christ. To Luther the revelation of God in Christ was the key to everything, and the significance of this revelation was to be found on the cross. 'God does not want to be known except through Christ; nor can he be known in any other way', he wrote in 1535. To Luther, God was *Deus crucifixus*, the crucified God.

The celebration in 1883 of the 400th anniversary of Luther's birth (which happened to be the year Studdert Kennedy was born) led to a 'rediscovery' of Luther. The publication of the Weimar edition of his works, many hitherto unpublished, led to an explosion of Luther scholarship and the resurgence of his ideas about the God 'hidden in suffering'. It also gave a final impetus to the 'history of dogma' movement, which reached its climax at the end of the nineteenth century, which was concerned with eliminating numerous Greek ideas – such as the impassibility of God – that had found their way into Christian theology.

A Twentieth-Century 'Theology of the Cross'

We can assume that Studdert Kennedy came into contact with this Lutheran revival during his time at Ripon Clergy College in

1907-8, but what is certain is that it came into the view of another young theologian, born three years after Studdert Kennedy in 1886, whose name was Karl Barth.

Karl Barth

Barth (1886-1968) is generally regarded as the founder of neo-orthodoxy. He argued that God's supreme self-revelation to the world has taken place in Jesus Christ. He is the 'Wholly Other', God breaking into our world of time and space, an irruption into this world of another and wholly different One. In Jesus God comes to us in a form with which we are familiar, taking upon himself our humanity in its weakness, need and sin. In *The Epistle to the Romans*, first published in 1918, Barth writes:

> Jesus stands among sinners as a sinner; He sets Himself wholly under the judgement under which the world is set; He takes His place where God can be present only in questioning about Him; He takes the form of a slave; He moves to the cross and to death; His greatest achievement is a negative achievement. He is not a genius, endowed with manifest or even occult powers; He is not a hero or leader of men. (Barth 1968:97)

For Barth, the notion of the omnipotence of God must always be understood in the light of God's self-revelation in Christ, a principle that found further expression at the hands of Dietrich Bonhoeffer, who studied under Barth in Bonn in 1931.

Dietrich Bonhoeffer

Bonhoeffer (1906-45) famously took up this discourse about Christ as 'this weak man among sinners' in a series of lectures on Christology in 1933. Writing later during his incarceration in Tegel Prison in Berlin in 1944 he wrote:

God lets himself be pushed out of the world on to the cross. He is weak and powerless in the world, and that is precisely the way, the only way, in which he is with us and helps us. Matt[hew] 8.17 makes it quite clear that Christ helps us, not by virtue of his omnipotence, but by virtue of his weakness and suffering. (Bonhoeffer 2001:134)

Expounding a kenotic Christology in tune with that of Studdert Kennedy, Bonhoeffer links the suffering of God to his weakness and powerlessness. Christ came to us in weakness not in strength, in gentleness, love and humility. This is a God of abundant, vulnerable and suffering love, who suffered rejection and hatred, loneliness and despair, agonizing pain and death – 'even death on a cross' (Philippians 2.8) – not an Almighty God at all. As Klemens von Klemperer affirms it:

God as he [Bonhoeffer] saw him, was not God almighty, but weak and powerless in this world. He is the suffering God, the God 'hidden in suffering' (Luther), the God on the cross. And man is called upon to suffer the grief together with God. It is not the religious act that makes the Christian, but partici-pation in the suffering of God. (von Klemperer 1998:96)

Bonhoeffer was hanged at Flossenbürg concentration camp on 9 April 1945 for the stand he made against Nazi tyranny and the extermination of the Jews, a suffering of humanity on such a horrific scale that it was to play its own important part in the development of a theology of a suffering God.

Holocaust Theology
In a famous tale of Auschwitz, the Holocaust survivor Elie Wiesel recounts in his memoir *Night* the day that a young boy, 'the sad-eyed angel', was hanged on the gallows – an event the other prisoners were made to watch:

Behind me, I heard the same man asking: "For God's sake, where is God?" And from within me, I heard a voice answer: "Where He is? This is where – hanging here from this gallows." (Wiesel 2006:65)

As a Jew, Wiesel is unable to make the connection with Christ on the cross. For him God was not on the gallows in the midst of human suffering, suffering with humanity and taking upon himself all under which it suffers. For him God was *really* dead, his Judaic faith was lost, and he now faced life alone in a world without God. The God of his ancestors and the faith of his childhood had vanished forever in the smoke of the crematoria. In a foreword to the book by François Mauriac, a Christian, Mauriac recalls a meeting with Wiesel and ponders what he might have said to him:

What did I say to him? Did I speak to him of that other Jew, this crucified brother who perhaps resembled him and whose cross conquered the world? Did I explain to him that what had been a stumbling block for *his* faith had become a cornerstone for *mine*? And that the connection between the cross and human suffering remains, in my view, the key to the unfathomable mystery in which the faith of his childhood was lost... But all I could do was embrace him and weep. (Mauriac in Wiesel 2006:xxi)

When the full extent of the unspeakable tragedy of the Holocaust came to the world's attention, it was to give further impetus to the development of a twentieth-century theology of the cross, most notably at the hands of Jürgen Moltmann.

Jürgen Moltmann

In a preface to Moltmann's *The Crucified God*, first published in 1972, Richard Bauckham writes:

The Crucified God could be said to be about believing in God 'after Auschwitz', where Auschwitz stands, without surrendering its own particular reality, for all the horrors of twentieth-century history. (Bauckham in Moltmann 2001:ix)

It was as a prisoner-of-war in England and Scotland during the Second World War that Moltmann (b. 1926) was first confronted with the repugnant truth of the Holocaust and became concerned for the first time with questions of Christian faith and theology in actual life. For him, an impassible God is a useless and pointless God. A God who cannot suffer must also be a God incapable of loving, for limitless and self-giving love is vulnerable and must be prepared one day to be wounded. He also sees the classical idea of the omnipotence of God as the cause of 'protest atheism', atheism which does not doubt the existence of God in itself but does doubt whether an unjust world of triumphant evil and suffering without end can possibly be grounded in and guided by a good and righteous God:

The only way past protest atheism is through a theology of the cross which understands God as the suffering God in the suffering of Christ and which cries out with the godforsaken God, 'My God, why have you forsaken me?' (Moltmann 2001:234)

The Crucified God is widely regarded as the most significant and influential work to have expounded the theology of a suffering God, and is credited with bringing a theology of the cross to its fullest expression and acceptance. In a later work, *The Trinity and the Kingdom of God*, Moltmann attributes to Studdert Kennedy a more seminal role than Barth in the development of this 'new orthodoxy' in Christian thought:

His book *The Hardest Part* has a prophetic and radical force rather like that of Barth's *Epistle to the Romans*, which came out at about the same time. In fact it deserved even greater attention than Barth's book, for the theology of the suffering God is more important than the theology of the God who is 'Wholly Other'. What was able to stand the test of the battle-fields of Flanders and created faith even in the hells there was the discovery of the crucified God. (Moltmann 1981:35)

What better reply could there be to the critics of his day? To be fair, they could not have foreseen what was to ensue: they had not yet encountered Barth, and they believed they had seen 'the war to end all wars'. Another World War and the Holocaust were still to come, and they would give new impetus to a twentieth-century theology of the cross to which Studdert Kennedy had given life.

Studdert Kennedy's ministry ran its course through the poverty of the Edwardian era, the appalling loss of life of the 1914-18 war, and the disillusion and depression of the 1920s which followed. In his opposition to suffering, however caused, he played an influential part in the development of a new theodicy that sought to protest against evil and create a motive to overcome it:

His concern with it [evil] was two-fold: How to believe in and love God in spite of it; and how to get rid of it. He saw that these two questions are at root the same. For if it cannot be got rid of, that argues some fatal defect in the Creator. But if it can, then the process of getting rid of it will be the means of revealing the perfected glory of God. (Temple 1929:219)

He saw as abhorrent any attempt to justify evil and suffering as being God-willed and of divine purpose (Irenaeus), and saw as inadequate the 'free will defence' (Augustine/Aquinas) because it portrayed God as being untouched or untroubled by the suffering of his creation. It did not take account of the God who suffers in, with and for his creation, nor did it say anything about what Christ is meant to have revealed of God's nature. He realized that these attempts to justify or defend God's action or inaction in the world would only distance people further from God, and that the question the theologian ought to be asking is 'where can we actually see God himself in the midst of all this evil and suffering?' Studdert Kennedy saw God present in the muddy, bloody hero in the trenches of the Western Front. In this act of solidarity with all human suffering there is the cry of God himself joining in the protest of humanity against him, 'My God, my God, why have you forsaken me?' (Matthew 27.46). And in this protest, there is no passive acquiescence with evil and suffering but rather a call to overcome it, to seek the future in which the will of God will be fulfilled:

Passionately fierce the voice of God is pleading,
    Pleading with men to arm them for the fight;
See how those hands, majestically bleeding,
    Call us to rout the armies of the night.
(Studdert Kennedy 1927:3)

To be afflicted by evil is not to be afflicted by God but to be appointed in Christ to join God's fight to conquer evil wherever it is to be found.

Some years ago I spent a few months on placement in another parish whose 'mission statement' was 'to know God and to make Him known in wonder, love and praise'. I became interested in finding out *how* they know God and how they speak about God when making him known to others, with a view to understanding what knowledge and language about God is being passed down to a new generation. So I set about asking the Sunday School leaders and the parents of the Sunday School children: 'What words do you use when speaking about God?'

The most commonly-used adjectives were 'loving', 'forgiving', 'merciful' and 'gracious', followed by 'powerful', 'almighty', 'awesome' and 'strong'. Out of 28 adjectives used when speaking about God, words such as 'weak', 'powerless', 'crucified' or 'suffering' made no appearance at all. It came as no surprise, therefore, to find the same pattern repeated when I asked the children themselves the same question. The conundrum of God, who is at the same time both all-loving and all-powerful, appears once more and bids us solve 'the problem of evil'.

If it is true that the Christian faith is struggling to show itself to be relevant to so many young people today, it might also be true that one of the reasons for this struggle is that we are too often using the wrong language about God. The very real danger in the face of modern-day tragedies such as 9/11, the 2004 Asian tsunami and the 2011 Japanese earthquake and tsunami, is that our children will be sent down the road of 'protest atheism' as described by Moltmann. Instead of finding God in the picking-up-the-pieces and the rebuilding of people's lives, instead of protesting against evil and suffering and finding a motive to overcome it, they will simply be blaming God and turning away from God because they have come to misunderstand his nature and his purposes – much as Charles Darwin did.

This is the relevance of a theology of the cross to the ministry and mission of the Church today. Just as Israel discerned God in its apparent abandonment by God in the crisis of the exile, there also will God be found today. The further we are led into life's hard places, into the depths of human despair and suffering, the closer we are drawn into the mystery of a suffering God, and the motifs of cross and resurrection will continually echo.

About the Author

The Reverend Tim Heaton is in parish ministry in the Diocese of Salisbury. He was ordained as a Deacon in 2008 and Priest in 2010 at the age of 51. That same year, he was awarded a BA (Honours) Degree in Theology for Christian Ministry and Mission. Educated at Harrow and Sandhurst, he spent five years in the army before pursuing a career in the City of London. After twenty years he left the City in 2003 to answer his call to ordination. He lives in north Dorset with his wife Arabella.

Bibliography

All scripture quotations are from the *New Revised Standard Version* unless stated otherwise.

Barth, K. (1968) *The Epistle to the Romans* (translated from the 6th edition), Oxford: OUP.

Bauckham, R. and Hart, T. (1999) *Hope against Hope: Christian Eschatology in Contemporary Context*, London: Darton, Longman and Todd.

Bonhoeffer, D. (2001) *Letters and Papers from Prison: An Abridged Edition*, London: SCM Press.

Darwin, C. R. (1998) *The Origin of Species* (reprinted from the 1st edition of 1859) with an Introduction by Jeff Wallace, Ware: Wordsworth Editions.

Davies, P. (1990) *God and the New Physics*, Harmondsworth: Penguin.

Dennett, D. C. (1995) *Darwin's Dangerous Idea*, New York: Simon and Schuster.

Donovan, V. J. (1982) *Christianity Rediscovered: An Epistle from the Masai*, London: SCM Press.

Grundy, M. (1997) *A Fiery Glow in the Darkness: Woodbine Willie, Padre and Poet*, Worcester: Osborne Books.

Hart, T. (1995) *Faith Thinking: The Dynamics of Christian Theology*, London: SPCK.

Hawking, S. and Mlodinow, L. (2010) *The Grand Design*, London: Bantam Press.

Miller, K. R. (2002) *Finding Darwin's God: A Scientist's Search for Common Ground Between God and Evolution*, New York: Harper Perennial.

Moltmann, J. (1981) *The Trinity and the Kingdom of God: The Doctrine of God*, London: SCM Press.

Moltmann, J. (2001) *The Crucified God: The Cross of Christ as the Foundation and Criticism of Christian Theology*, London: SCM Press.

Polkinghorne, J. (1988) *Science and Creation: The Search for Understanding*, London: SPCK.

Purcell, W. (1983) *Woodbine Willie: A Study of Geoffrey Studdert Kennedy* (2nd edition), Oxford: Mowbray.

Rittner, C., Smith, S. D. and Steinfeldt, I. eds. (2000) *The Holocaust and the Christian World*, New York: Continuum.

Spencer, N. (2009) *Darwin and God*, London: SPCK.

Studdert Kennedy, G. A. (2007/1918) *The Hardest Part*, Liskeard: Diggory Press.

Studdert Kennedy, G. A. (1927) *The Unutterable Beauty: The Collected Poetry of G. A. Studdert Kennedy*, London: Hodder and Stoughton.

Temple, W. (1929) 'Studdert Kennedy: The Man and his Message' in Mozley, J. K. ed. *G. A. Studdert Kennedy: By His Friends*, London: Hodder and Stoughton.

The Archbishops' Council (2000) *Common Worship: Services and Prayers for the Church of England*, London: Church House Publishing.

The United Reformed Church (2003) *Worship: from The United Reformed Church*, London: The United Reformed Church.

Vanstone, W. H. (1977) *Love's Endeavour, Love's Expense: The Response of Being to the Love of God*, London: Darton, Longman and Todd.

von Klemperer, K. (1998) 'Totalitarianism and resistance in Germany: Dietrich Bonhoeffer' in Chandler, A. ed. *The Terrible Alternative*, London: Cassell.

Ward, K. (1998) *God, Faith & the New Millennium: Christian Belief in an Age of Science*, Oxford: Oneworld.

Ware, K. (1995) *The Orthodox Way* (Revised edition), Crestwood NY: St Vladimir's Seminary Press.

Wiesel, E. (2006) *Night*, London: Penguin Books.

Williams, R. (2002) *Writing in the Dust: Reflections on 11th September and its aftermath*, London: Hodder & Stoughton.

Winstone, H. ed. (1977) *The Sunday Missal* (Revised edition), London: Collins.

Wright, N. T. (2006) *New Heavens, New Earth: The Biblical Picture of Christian Hope* (2nd edition), Cambridge: Grove Books.

Websites

The Complete Works of Charles Darwin Online can be found at:
<www.darwin-online.org.uk>

Darwin Correspondence Project can be found at:
<www.darwinproject.ac.uk>

Public domain books can be found through Google Book Search
at:
<http://books.google.com>

Circle Books

Circle is a symbol of infinity and unity. It's part of a growing list of imprints, including o-books.net and zero-books.net.

Circle Books aims to publish books in Christian spirituality that are fresh, accessible, and stimulating.

Our books are available in all good English language bookstores worldwide. If you can't find the book on the shelves, then ask your bookstore to order it for you, quoting the ISBN and title. Or, you can order online—all major online retail sites carry our titles.

To see our list of titles, please view www.Circle-Books.com, growing by 80 titles per year.

Authors can learn more about our proposal process by going to our website and clicking on Your Company > Submissions.

We define Christian spirituality as the relationship between the self and its sense of the transcendent or sacred, which issues in literary and artistic expression, community, social activism, and practices. A wide range of disciplines within the field of religious studies can be called upon, including history, narrative studies, philosophy, theology, sociology, and psychology. Interfaith in approach, Circle Books fosters creative dialogue with non-Christian traditions.

And tune into MySpiritRadio.com for our book review radio show, hosted by June-Elleni Laine, where you can listen to authors discussing their books.

MySpiritRadio